From our Kitchen to Yours

Our Best
5-INGREDIENT
Fresh Family Recipes

Easy, healthy dishes everyone will love!

D1512104

To cooks everywhere who want to create easy & delicious meals for their family & friends.

Gooseberry Patch
An imprint of Globe Pequot
246 Goose Lane
Guilford, CT 06437

www.gooseberrypatch.com
1 800 854 6673

••••••••••••••••••••••

Do you have a tried & true recipe... tip, craft or memory that you'd like to see featured in a **Gooseberry Patch** cookbook? Visit our website at www.gooseberrypatch.com and follow the easy steps to submit your favorite family recipe.

Or send them to us at:
Gooseberry Patch
PO Box 812
Columbus, OH 43216-0812

Don't forget to include the number of servings your recipe makes, plus your name, address, phone number and email address. If we select your recipe, your name will appear right along with it... and you'll receive a FREE copy of the book!

CONTENTS

Make it Easy...Make it Tasty...Make it Healthy

Food that is good for you can also be yummy and easy to make. In this book, you'll find more than 200 recipes that are made with 5 ingredients or less. We have also given you the nutritional analysis, so you can make good choices about what you make for your family. That's right...easy, tasty and healthy. You can have it all!

The Recipes:

The recipes in this book were chosen or developed to be lighter and healthier than some of the recipes you may have used in the past. This means they may have fewer calories, less fast, less salt and more fiber. We have chosen recipes that have lots of flavor and yet only have 5 ingredients or less.

Nutritional Analysis:

At the bottom of each recipe, you will see that the recipes have been analyzed to determine the nutritional content of the recipe. To help you understand what the values mean in these nutritional analyses, we recommend that you compare them with the FDA's recommended values. The chart, right, displays recommendations for an adult eating a 2000-calorie per day diet. You can refer to these numbers as you are looking at the nutritional values of the recipes in this book. Of course, if you are a larger or active person, you probably have higher nutritional needs, and if you are a smaller or sedentary person, you probably have lower nutritional needs. In addition, children, and pregnant and lactating women have unique nutritional needs.

FDA Daily Recommendations for the Average American Adult	
Total Calories	2000 calories
Total Fat	65g
Saturated Fat	20g
Cholesterol	300g
Sodium	2400mg
Carbohydrates	300g
Fiber	25g
Protein	50g

Note that ingredients in a product can vary slightly according to brands and natural differences in ingredients. The nutritional analyses were based on typical brands and ingredients of products available.

When calculating the nutritional analysis, we considered these things: If the recipe calls for a specific amount of salt or pepper, these were included in the nutritional analysis. If it calls for salt and pepper to taste, then it was not. If an ingredient was optional or a garnish, it was not included in the nutritional analysis. If there was a marinade or dressing, we based the nutritional analysis on what was actually used per serving, not including any extra leftover sauce or dressing.

Only 5 Ingredients:
To be sure the recipes are quick & easy to make, we have chosen recipes with only 5 ingredients or less. When we chose the recipes and counted the ingredients, we did not include salt, pepper, oil or water. Sometimes we included optional ingredients that you could add that would make the recipe have a few more ingredients. Whichever you choose, you can be sure the recipes will be delicious and please your family and friends.

Toasty Tomato Sandwich, p. 22

CHAPTER ONE

GOOD MORNING
Breakfasts &
Breads

Melon-Berry Bowls, p. 18

No-Crust Spinach Quiche, p. 12

Kathy Grashoff, Fort Wayne, IN

Kathy's Bacon Popover

Mmm...bacon! An easy tote-along breakfast to enjoy on the go.

Makes one dozen, serves 12

2 eggs
1 c. skim milk
1 T. oil
1/2 c. all-purpose flour
1/2 c. whole-wheat flour
1/2 t. salt
2 slices bacon, crisply cooked and
   crumbled

Whisk together eggs, milk and oil. Beat in flours and salt just until smooth. Fill 12 greased and floured muffin cups 2/3 full. Sprinkle crumbled bacon evenly over batter. Bake at 400 degrees for about 25 to 30 minutes, until puffed and golden. Serve warm.

Nutrition Per Serving: *74 calories, 3g total fat, 1g sat fat, 33mg cholesterol, 151mg sodium, 9g carbohydrate, 1g fiber, 4g protein*

Lynda Robson, Boston, MA

Overnight Cherry Oatmeal

Assemble the night before and wake to the aroma of cherry pie...what a great way to start the day!

Serves 6

3 c. long-cooking oats, uncooked
3/4 c. powdered sugar
1/4 t. salt
3/4 c. frozen tart cherries, drained
6 c. water
Optional: 1 t. almond extract

Combine oats, powdered sugar and salt in a large bowl; pour into a slow cooker that has been sprayed with non-stick vegetable spray. Add remaining ingredients; stir until combined. Cover and cook on low setting for 7 to 8 hours.

Nutrition Per Serving: *221 calories, 2g total fat, 0g sat fat, 0mg cholesterol, 100mg sodium, 45g carbohydrate, 5g fiber, 6g protein*

GOOD TO KNOW
Oatmeal is a carbohydrate that can help maintain glucose levels. However, avoid prepackaged or instant oatmeal. These products can contain unexpected sugar and artificial flavorings.

Overnight Cherry Oatmeal

Elizabeth Holcomb, Canyon Lake, TX

Texas Toads in the Hole

I made this recipe for my girls when they were little. They always loved it because of the funny name, as well as the fact they had eggs and toast all in one dish!

Serves 4

2 T. butter
4 thick slices whole-grain bread
4 eggs
salt and pepper to taste
Optional: jam, jelly or preserves

Spread butter on both sides of bread. Using a biscuit cutter, cut a circle out of the middle of each slice of bread; set aside rounds. Place bread slices in a large, lightly greased skillet over medium heat; break an egg into each hole. Season with salt and pepper. Cook until egg white begins to set, then carefully flip. Continue to cook until eggs reach desired doneness. In a separate skillet, toast reserved bread rounds. Top rounds with jam, jelly or preserves, if desired. Serve with bread slices.

Nutrition Per Serving: *175 calories, 8g total fat, 4g sat fat, 15mg cholesterol, 228mg sodium, 18g carbohydrate, 3g fiber, 9g protein*

Rebekah Spooner, Huntsville, AL

Johnny Appleseed Toast

I'm a teacher, and we make this every fall to celebrate Johnny Appleseed with our little ones in September. It also makes a wonderfully quick fall breakfast when you serve it with Cheddar cheese slices and cold milk.

Makes 4 servings

4 slices cinnamon-raisin bread
1-1/2 T. butter, divided
1 Gala apple, cored and sliced
4 t. honey
1 t. cinnamon

Spread each slice of bread with one teaspoon of butter. Cover each bread slice with an apple slice; drizzle with one teaspoon honey and sprinkle with cinnamon. Place topped bread slices on an ungreased baking sheet. Broil on high for one to 2 minutes, until toasted and golden.

Nutrition Per Serving: *155 calories, 6g total fat, 3g sat fat, 11mg cholesterol, 103mg sodium, 26g carbohydrate, 3g fiber, 2g protein*

Johnny Appleseed Toast

Beth Kramer, Port Saint Lucie, FL

Strawberry-Hazelnut Grits

This combination of strawberry, cocoa and hazelnut is just too yummy to pass up!

Serves 2

3/4 c. quick-cooking grits, uncooked
1 T. butter
3 T. chocolate-hazelnut spread
6 to 7 strawberries, hulled and
    chopped

Prepare grits according to package directions. Stir in butter and chocolate-hazelnut spread. Fold in strawberries.

Nutrition Per Serving: *431 calories, 15g total fat, 12g sat fat, 15mg cholesterol, 13mg sodium, 67g carbohydrate, 3g fiber, 7g protein*

> GOOD TO KNOW
> **A staple for centuries, corn is brimming with good-for-you nutrients, including carbohydrates, vitamins and fiber.**

Mary Mayall, Dracut, MA

No-Crust Spinach Quiche

If you want meat in this dish, add chopped ham or crumbled bacon to this delicious crustless quiche.

Serves 6

10-oz. pkg. frozen chopped spinach,
    thawed and drained
Optional: 1/2 c. onion or
    mushrooms, chopped
6 eggs, beaten
1/2 c. milk
1 c. shredded Swiss or Cheddar
    cheese

Spread spinach in a greased 9" pie plate. Sprinkle with onion and/or mushrooms, if desired. Beat together eggs and milk; stir in cheese. Pour egg mixture evenly over spinach. Bake at 350 degrees for 25 to 35 minutes, until top is golden and a knife tip inserted into center comes out clean. Cool slightly before cutting.

Nutrition Per Serving: *171 calories, 12g total fat, 6g sat fat, 233mg cholesterol, 230mg sodium, 4g carbohydrate, 1g fiber, 13g protein*

No-Crust Spinach Quiche

Patricia Reitz, Winchester, VA

Blueberry Flaxseed Smoothies

This oh-so-healthy smoothie is just as pretty as it is delicious!

Serves 4

1 banana, cut into chunks
1/2 c. blueberries
1 c. low-fat vanilla yogurt
1 c. fat-free milk
2 T. ground flaxseed
Garnish: fresh strawberries,
   blueberries, flaxseed

Combine all ingredients except garnish in a blender; process on high setting until smooth. Pour into glasses. Garnish with fruit and flaxseed.

Nutrition Per Serving: *127 calories, 2g total fat, 1g sat fat, 5mg cholesterol, 73mg sodium, 21g carbohydrate, 2g fiber, 5g protein*

Crystal Shook, Catawba, NC

Peanutty Take-Along Wrap

In a hurry every morning? Don't leave home without breakfast! These make it easy and yummy.

Makes 2 servings

8-inch whole-wheat tortilla
1 T. creamy peanut butter
1 T. vanilla yogurt
Optional: 1 t. honey
1/4 c. granola
1/4 c. blueberries

Spread one side of tortilla with peanut butter and yogurt. Drizzle with honey, if desired; sprinkle with granola and fruit. Roll up tightly and cut in half. Serve immediately, or wrap tightly in plastic wrap and refrigerate.

Nutrition Per Serving: *197 calories, 8g total fat, 2g sat fat, 0mg cholesterol, 149mg sodium, 28g carbohydrate, 3g fiber, 6g protein*

KITCHEN TIP
Spray a measuring cup with non-stick vegetable spray before measuring honey, marshmallow creme or peanut butter...the sticky stuff will slip right out.

Peanutty Take-Along Wrap

Sonya Labbe, Quebec, Canada

Ham & Gruyère Egg Cup

This recipe is always on our Sunday brunch table. It is quick, easy and tasty...very pretty too!

Serves 12

12 thin slices deli ham
3/4 c. shredded Gruyère cheese
1 doz. eggs
salt and pepper to taste
3/4 c. milk
2 T. grated Parmesan cheese
Garnish: pepper

Spray 12 muffin cups or ramekins with non-stick vegetable spray. Line each muffin cup or ramekin with a slice of ham folded in half. Top each ham slice with one tablespoon Gruyère cheese, an egg cracked into the cup, a sprinkle of salt and pepper, one tablespoon milk and 1/2 teaspoon Parmesan cheese. Place muffin tin or ramekins on a baking sheet. Bake at 450 degrees for 15 minutes, or until eggs are set. If using a muffin tin, allow baked eggs to cool several minutes before removing them from the muffin tin. Cool slightly before serving in ramekins. Sprinkle with pepper.

Nutrition Per Serving: *133 calories, 9g total fat, 4g sat fat, 230mg cholesterol, 268mg sodium, 1g carbohydrate, 0g fiber, 12g protein*

Victoria Mitchel, Gettysburg, PA

Mile-High Biscuits

The buttermilk in these biscuits make them so light and tender!

Makes 12 servings

2 c. all-purpose flour
4 t. baking powder
1/4 t. baking soda
3/4 t. salt
5 T. chilled butter, diced
1 c. buttermilk

Combine flour, baking powder, baking soda and salt in a food processor; add butter. Pulse just until mixture resembles coarse crumbs. Transfer mixture to a large bowl; add buttermilk. Stir until mixture begins to hold together. Turn out onto a lightly floured surface. Working quickly, knead until most of the dough sticks together. Pat out dough into a 12" circle, 1/2" thick. Cut with a biscuit cutter, quickly re-gathering dough until about 12 biscuits are cut. Arrange biscuits in a parchment paper-lined 13"x9" baking pan. Set pan on center oven rack. Bake at 450 degrees for about 10 minutes, until lightly golden. Serve warm.

Nutrition Per Serving: *117 calories, 4g total fat, 3g sat fat, 13mg cholesterol, 416mg sodium, 16g carbohydrate, 0g fiber, 3g protein*

Mile-High Biscuits

Karen Puchnick, Butler, PA

Crispy Corn Fritters

So easy to make...delicious with a pasta salad!

Makes 8 servings

1 c. biscuit baking mix
1/2 c. milk
1 egg
1 c. frozen corn, thawed
pepper to taste
2 T. oil
Optional: honey

In a bowl, stir together baking mix, milk and egg until just blended. Stir in corn; season with pepper. Let batter stand for 5 to 10 minutes. Heat oil in a skillet over medium heat. Drop batter into oil with a large spoon. Cook until golden; turn and cook one minute on the other side. Drain on paper towels. Serve drizzled with a little honey, if desired.

Nutrition Per Serving: *130 calories, 7g total fat, 1g sat fat, 28mg cholesterol, 220mg sodium, 15g carbohydrate, 1g fiber, 3g protein*

Jill Ball, Highland, UT

Melon-Berry Bowls

I am always looking for quick, healthy and yummy breakfast ideas for my teenagers. This one has become a favorite!

Serves 3

1 honeydew melon, halved and
   seeded
6-oz. container favorite-flavor
   yogurt
1/2 c. blueberries
1 c. granola cereal
Garnish: orange slice

Use a melon baller to scoop honeydew into balls. Combine melon balls with remaining ingredients except garnish. Spoon into individual bowls. Garnish with orange slice.

Nutrition Per Serving: *342 calories, 3g total fat, 1g sat fat, 3mg cholesterol, 186mg sodium, 77g carbohydrate, 6g fiber, 8g protein*

GOOD TO KNOW
Honeydew melon is beautiful in that bowl of fruit, and it is also rich in potassium and vitamin C as well as vitamin K, B6 and folate.

Melon-Berry Bowls

Vickie, Gooseberry Patch

Mocha Coffee

Keep this coffee mix on hand for those busy mornings when you want a rich cup of java.

Makes 10 servings

6 T. plus 2 t. instant espresso coffee powder
1-1/4 c. fat-free powdered non-dairy creamer
1/2 c. plus 2 t. sugar
3 T. plus 1 t. baking cocoa
1 T. vanilla powder

Combine all ingredients, stirring well. Store in an airtight container. For each serving, add 3/4 cup boiling water to 1/4 cup mix; stir well.

Nutrition Per Serving: *104 calories, 0g total fat, 0g sat fat, 0mg cholesterol, 30mg sodium, 23g carbohydrate, 1g fiber, 0g protein*

Holly Meurisse, Salt Lake City, UT

Irish Soda Bread

So simple and dense, this old-world quick bread is perfect with fried eggs and ham.

Makes 2 small loaves, serves 4

1-1/2 c. whole wheat flour
1 c. all-purpose flour
1/2 t. baking soda
2 t. sugar
1 t. salt
1-1/4 c. buttermilk

Combine dry ingredients in a large bowl. Add enough buttermilk to make a soft dough. Knead on lightly floured board for about 2 minutes. Form into 2 round loaves. Cut a cross in the middle of each loaf. Place loaves on a greased baking sheet. Bake at 375 degrees for 20 to 30 minutes until golden.

Nutrition Per Serving: *305 calories, 2g total fat, 0g sat fat, 3mg cholesterol, 815mg sodium, 61g carbohydrate, 7g fiber, 12g protein*

KITCHEN TIP
Keep your whole-wheat flour in the freezer to keep it fresh until you are ready to make that special bread.

Irish Soda Bread

Nancy Wise, Little Rock, AR

Honey Fruit Yogurt Dip

We make this recipe to have for a quick breakfast treat with favorite fruits. The honey in the dip gives it just the right amount of sweetness.

Serves 6

1-1/3 c. non-fat plain Greek yogurt
2 t. honey
1/4 t. orange zest
1 T. orange juice
1/8 t. vanilla extract

Stir together all ingredients in a serving bowl. Cover and chill.

Nutrition Per Serving: *47 calories, 0g total fat, 0g sat fat, 4mg cholesterol, 31mg sodium, 5g carbohydrate, 0g fiber, 7g protein*

Jan Temeyer, Polk City, IA

Toasty Tomato Sandwich

Fresh heirloom tomatoes make this a show-stopper for a quick summer breakfast. We really love brioche bread...it is also yummy with whole-grain or rye bread.

Serves 4

4 slices brioche bread
1 T. mayonnaise
1 T. fresh basil, chopped
4 slices fresh tomato
1/4 c. grated Parmesan cheese
Garnish: pea sprouts, pepper

Toast bread and place on baking sheet. Mix together mayonnaise and basil; spread on the toast. Place one tomato slice on each piece of bread and sprinkle with cheese. Broil in oven for about one minute or until cheese is melted. Garnish with sprouts and pepper, if desired. Serve immediately.

Nutrition Per Serving: *128 calories, 5g total fat, 1g sat fat, 5mg cholesterol, 265mg sodium, 16g carbohydrate, 1g fiber, 5g protein*

Toasty Tomato Sandwich

Connie Pritt, Coalton, WV

Orange Slush

Refresh yourself every morning with a glass of soothing orange goodness made from frozen orange juice.

Serves 2

6-oz. can frozen orange juice
   concentrate
1 c. milk
1 t. vanilla extract
12 ice cubes

Place all ingredients in blender; blend to desired consistency. Pour into glasses

Nutrition Per Serving: *236 calories, 2g total fat, 1g sat fat, 10mg cholesterol, 53mg sodium, 47g carbohydrate, 1g fiber, 7g protein*

GOOD TO KNOW
Orange juice packs a punch of vitamin C and is considered one of the best sources of this essential vitamin.

Nicole Millard, Mendon, MI

Grandma McKindley's Waffles

You can't go wrong with an old-fashioned waffle breakfast...the topping choices are endless!

Makes 10 waffles

2 c. all-purpose flour
1 T. baking powder
1/4 t. salt
2 eggs, separated
1-1/2 c. milk
3 T. butter, melted
Garnish: fresh berries, maple syrup

Sift together flour, baking powder and salt; set aside. With an electric mixer on high speed, beat egg whites until stiff; set aside. Stir egg yolks, milk and melted butter together and add to flour mixture, stirring just until moistened. Fold in egg whites. Ladle batter by 1/2 cupfuls onto a lightly greased preheated waffle iron; bake according to manufacturer's directions. Garnish as desired.

Nutrition Per Serving: *154 calories, 5g total fat, 3g sat fat, 54mg cholesterol, 231mg sodium, 21g carbohydrate, 1g fiber, 5g protein*

Grandma McKindley's Waffles

Linda Behling, Cecil, PA

Chai Tea

This quick-to-make tea gets you off to a great start with just a little spice.

Serves 20

1 c. non-fat dry milk powder
1 c. powdered non-dairy creamer
1/2 c. sugar
Optional: 1 t. cardamom, 2 t. ground
   ginger
1 t. ground cloves
brewed black tea

In a large bowl, combine all ingredients except tea. To serve, add 2 tablespoons of mixture to one cup of brewed tea.

Nutrition Per Serving: *54 calories, 1g total fat, 0g sat fat, 0mg cholesterol, 19mg sodium, 9g carbohydrate, 0g fiber, 1g protein*

Michelle Case, Yardley, PA

Breakfast Berry Parfait

Choose a humble bowl or a pretty glass dish to present this super-easy breakfast. Choose the flavor of yogurt that your family loves...it all tastes so good!

Makes 3 servings

1/2 c. strawberries, hulled
1/2 c. raspberries
1/4 c. blackberries
1/2 c. blueberries
6-oz. container low-fat strawberry
   yogurt
Garnish: Toasted coconut, toasted
   sliced almonds

Combine berries in a bowl. Spoon yogurt over berry mixture. Garnish with coconut and almonds.

Nutrition Per Serving: *86 calories, 1g total fat, 0g sat fat, 3mg cholesterol, 38mg sodium, 17g carbohydrate, 3g fiber, 4g protein*

Breakfast Berry Parfait

Shiri Parsons, Cape Carteret, NC

Banana-Mango Soy Smoothies

This smoothie starts your day off right!

Serves 6

2 c. vanilla or plain soy milk
2 to 3 bananas, sliced and frozen
6 mangoes, pitted, peeled, cubed and
    frozen
1 T. honey, or to taste

Combine all ingredients in a blender. Blend on high setting until smooth and frothy. Pour into tall glasses.

Nutrition Per Serving: *225 calories, 2g total fat, 0g sat fat, 0mg cholesterol, 33mg sodium, 54g carbohydrate, 5g fiber, 3g protein*

Jo Ann, Gooseberry Patch

Cinnamon-Apple Quinoa Breakfast Bowls

You can serve the quinoa with or without the apples, but everyone we know loves the combination!

Makes 4 servings

1/2 c. quinoa, uncooked, rinsed and
    drained
1-1/4 c. almond milk
1/2 t. vanilla extract
1/4 t. cinnamon
1/8 t. nutmeg
1/8 t. salt
Optional: almond milk, chopped
    pecans, shredded coconut

Prepare Maple Roasted Apples, if using. Meanwhile, in a saucepan over medium heat, stir together quinoa, almond milk, vanilla, spices and salt. Bring to a boil; reduce heat to low. Simmer for 10 to 15 minutes, until quinoa is cooked through and liquid has been absorbed. Remove from heat; cover and let stand for 5 to 10 minutes. Fluff with a fork. To serve, divide warm quinoa among 4 bowls; top with apple mixture, if using. Garnish as desired.

Nutrition Per Serving: *98 calories, 2g total fat, 0g sat fat, 0mg cholesterol, 123mg sodium, 16g carbohydrate, 2g fiber, 3g protein*

MAPLE ROASTED APPLES:
1 T. coconut oil, melted
2 T. maple syrup
1/4 t. cinnamon
1/8 t. nutmeg
2 Gala apples, quartered and cored

In a bowl, whisk together coconut oil and maple syrup; stir in spices. Add apples; toss until coated. Arrange apples on a parchment paper-lined rimmed baking sheet. Bake at 375 degrees for 20 to 25 minutes, basting with pan juices once or twice, until golden. Cool slightly.

Nutrition Per Serving: *103 calories, 4g total fat, 3g sat fat, 0mg cholesterol, 2mg sodium, 19g carbohydrate, 2g fiber, 0g protein*

Cinnamon-Apple Quinoa Breakfast Bowls

April Haury, Paramus, NJ

Mom's Fruit Smoothies

This smoothie is so fresh and full of flavor.

Makes 3 servings

1-1/2 c. fresh or frozen peaches, cut into chunks
2 mangoes, pitted and diced
1 banana, cut into chunks
8-oz. container non-fat plain yogurt
1 T. honey

Combine all ingredients in a blender. Process until smooth; pour into tall glasses.

Nutrition Per Serving: *203 calories, 1g total fat, 0g sat fat, 2mg cholesterol, 59mg sodium, 49g carbohydrate, 3g fiber, 6g protein*

Christina Mendoza, Alamogordo, NM

California Omelet

We like this for a hearty breakfast, but omelets can make the quickest and tastiest dinners for the entire family...you can personalize each one to include favorite ingredients.

Serves 2

1 T. oil
3 to 4 eggs
1/4 c. milk
salt and pepper to taste
1 avocado, halved, pitted and sliced
Optional: 2 green onions, diced
1/2 c. shredded Monterey Jack cheese

Heat oil in a skillet over medium-low heat. Whisk together eggs, milk, salt and pepper in a bowl; pour into skillet. Cook until eggs are lightly golden on bottom and partially set on top. Sprinkle with remaining ingredients; carefully fold omelet in half so toppings are covered. Reduce heat to medium-low and cook, uncovered, about 5 to 10 minutes.

Nutrition Per Serving: *410 calories, 34g total fat, 10g sat fat, 346mg cholesterol, 294mg sodium, 9g carbohydrate, 5g fiber, 19g protein*

California Omelet

LaDeana Cooper, Batavia, OH

Farm-Fresh Omelet

As our garden started producing lots of veggies, my kids started making up their own recipes. For once, Mom was the assistant! Here is an all-time favorite that they came up with. We like our vegetables crisp, but if you prefer them more tender, sauté before adding to the omelet.

Makes one serving

2 eggs
1 T. skim milk
1/2 t. pepper
1/2 t. canola oil
1 T. asparagus, chopped into small
    pieces
1 T. carrot, cut into thin sticks
2 T. tomato, diced

Beat together eggs, milk and pepper in a bowl; set aside. Spray skillet with non-stick vegetable spray. Pour oil into a skillet over medium heat; add egg mixture. Cook until set underneath; flip gently and cook other side. Top half of omelet with vegetables. Fold over and turn out onto a plate.

Nutrition Per Serving: *178 calories, 12g total fat, 3g sat fat, 423mg cholesterol, 155mg sodium, 4g carbohydrate, 1g fiber, 14g protein*

Kelly Gray, Hedgesville, WV

Christmas Eggs

I used the eggs-in-a-hole idea for this recipe. My boys know it's Christmas when I start serving these eggs! They're so pretty on a plate at Christmastime, but fun to eat year 'round too. If you're not a fan of grits, you could serve them over buttered whole-grain toast.

Makes 6 servings

1 red pepper, sliced into 6, 1/4-inch
    thick rings
6 eggs
salt and pepper to taste
2 c. cooked grits
Garnish: chopped fresh parsley

Spray a large sauté pan or skillet generously with non-stick vegetable spray. Add red pepper rings and cook over medium-high heat, about 5 minutes on each side. Crack an egg into each pepper ring. Reduce heat to low. Cook to desired doneness, about 5 to 6 minutes. Season with salt and pepper. Use a spatula to remove eggs from pan and place one egg over a serving of grits in each bowl. Sprinkle with parsley.

Nutrition Per Serving: *125 calories, 5g total fat, 2g sat fat, 211mg cholesterol, 72mg sodium, 12g carbohydrate, 1g fiber, 8g protein*

Christmas Eggs

Jill Ball, Highland, UT

Apple Pie Oatmeal

This is an easy, healthy and hearty breakfast and so easy to make in the microwave.

Makes one serving

1 c. water
6 T. long-cooking oats, uncooked
1 t. brown sugar, packed
2 T. apple, peeled and diced
1/8 t. apple pie spice
Optional: milk

Combine water and oats in a microwave-safe bowl. Cover tightly with plastic wrap, folding back a small edge to allow steam to escape. Microwave on high for 2-1/2 minutes. Stir well. Top with remaining ingredients and milk, if desired.

Nutrition Per Serving: *149 calories, 2g total fat, 0g sat fat, 0mg cholesterol, 3mg sodium, 29g carbohydrate, 4g fiber, 4g protein*

Etha Hutchcroft, Ames, IA

Strawberry Preserves Smoothies

The sweetness of strawberry preserves is all the sugar you need to make a delicious, fresh and good-for-you smoothie.

Makes 4 servings

2 T. strawberry preserves
1 c. crushed pineapple in own juice
1 c. orange juice
3 c. fresh strawberries, hulled and sliced
16-oz. container low-fat plain yogurt

Combine all ingredients in a blender; process until smooth. Pour into chilled jelly jars to serve.

Nutrition Per Serving: *200 calories, 2g total fat, 1g sat fat, 6mg cholesterol, 85mg sodium, 40g carbohydrate, 3g fiber, 8g protein*

KITCHEN TIP
A photo album is just right for keeping frequently-used recipes handy on the kitchen counter. Tuck in a few photos of happy family mealtimes too!

Strawberry Preserves Smoothies

Lizzy Burnley, Ankeny, IA

Lizzy's Make-Ahead Egg Casserole

This recipe is a favorite for breakfast, lunch or dinner. And preparing it ahead makes it that much easier!

Serves 12

1 doz. eggs
1 c. cooked ham, diced
3 c. milk
12 frozen waffles
1/2 c. shredded Cheddar cheese

In a large bowl, beat eggs. Stir in ham and milk. Grease a 13"x9" baking pan. Place one layer of waffles in the bottom of the pan. Pour half of the mixture over waffles. Sprinkle with half of the cheese. Continue layering waffles, egg mixture and cheese.

Cover and refrigerate overnight. Uncover and bake at 350 degrees for about one hour, or until eggs are set.

Nutrition Per Serving: *246 calories, 12g total fat, 4g sat fat, 233mg cholesterol, 515mg sodium, 20g carbohydrate, 1g fiber, 14g protein*

Tina Butler, Royce City, TX

Fresh Spinach Smoothie

Fresh spinach gives this smoothie a beautiful green color and refreshing taste.

Makes 4 servings

1 c. vanilla almond milk
1 to 2 bananas, sliced and frozen
1 c. fresh spinach, torn into pieces,
　　stems removed
1/2 c. ice
Optional: 1 T. honey

Combine milk, bananas, spinach and ice in a blender; process on high setting until smooth. Add honey if a sweeter taste is desired. Pour into glasses to serve.

Nutrition Per Serving: *66 calories, 1g total fat, 0g sat fat, 0mg cholesterol, 51mg sodium, 14g carbohydrate, 2g fiber, 1g protein*

Fresh Spinach Smoothie

Julie Perkins, Anderson, IN

Peanut Butter French Toast

Who can resist the classic taste of peanut butter & jelly?

Serves 2

4 slices whole-grain bread
1/2 c. creamy peanut butter
1 T. grape jelly
3 eggs, beaten
1/4 c. milk
2 T. butter
Garnish: powdered sugar

Use bread, peanut butter and jelly to make 2 sandwiches; set aside. In a bowl, whisk together eggs and milk. Dip each sandwich into egg mixture. Melt butter in a non-stick skillet over medium heat. Add sandwiches to skillet and cook until golden, about 2 to 3 minutes on each side. Sprinkle with powdered sugar; cut diagonally into triangles.

Nutrition Per Serving: *768 calories, 54g total fat, 17g sat fat, 350mg cholesterol, 637mg sodium, 45g carbohydrate, 8g fiber, 34g protein*

Renae Scheiderer, Beallsville, OH

Festive Brunch Frittata

Peppers in bright colors make this frittata a pretty addition to your brunch table.

Makes 8 servings

8 eggs
1/8 t. salt
1/8 t. pepper
1/2 c. shredded reduced-fat Cheddar cheese
1 T. butter
2 c. red, green and yellow peppers, chopped
1/4 c. onion, chopped

Beat together eggs, salt and pepper. Fold in cheese and set aside. Spray a 10" non-stick, oven-proof skillet with non-stick vegetable spray. Melt butter in the skillet over medium-heat. Add peppers and onion to skillet; sauté until tender. Pour egg mixture over peppers and onion; do not stir. Reduce heat to medium-low. Cover and cook about 9 minutes, until eggs are set and frittata is lightly golden on the underside. Broil with top of frittata about 5 inches from heat for 5 minutes, or until lightly golden. Cut into wedges to serve.

Nutrition Per Serving: *108 calories, 7g total fat, 3g sat fat, 191mg cholesterol, 171mg sodium, 3g carbohydrate, 1g fiber, 8g protein*

Festive Brunch Frittata

Kristie Rigo, Friedens, PA

Blueberry Pillows

A delightful blend of cream cheese and blueberries is stuffed inside this French toast.

Serves 8

8-oz. pkg. cream cheese, softened
16 slices Italian bread
1/2 c. blueberries
2 eggs, beaten
1/2 c. milk
1 t. vanilla extract

Spread cream cheese evenly on 8 bread slices; arrange blueberries in a single layer over cream cheese. Top with remaining bread slices, gently pressing to seal; set aside. Whisk together eggs, milk and vanilla in a small bowl; brush over bread slices. Arrange on a greased hot griddle; cook until golden. Flip and cook other side until golden.

Nutrition Per Serving: *235 calories, 13g total fat, 6g sat fat, 85mg cholesterol, 347mg sodium, 23g carbohydrate, 1g fiber, 7g protein*

Amy Butcher, Columbus, GA

Fluffy Baked Eggs

Who would have thought to combine pineapple and eggs? After you taste this yummy recipe, you'll see why it is our family favorite!

Makes 12 servings

14 eggs, beaten
3 slices bacon, crisply cooked and crumbled
1-1/3 c. low-fat cottage cheese
8-oz. can crushed pineapple in own juice, drained
1 t. vanilla extract
Garnish: cooked bacon crumbles, chopped fresh parsley

Blend together eggs, bacon, cottage cheese, pineapple and vanilla; spoon into a greased 13"x9" baking pan. Bake, uncovered, at 350 degrees for 40 to 45 minutes, until center is set and a toothpick inserted in center comes out clean. Allow baking pan to stand 5 minutes before slicing. Garnish with cooked bacon crumbles and parsley if desired; cut into squares.

Nutrition Per Serving: *163 calories, 10g total fat, 3g sat fat, 227mg cholesterol, 261mg sodium, 4g carbohydrate, 0g fiber, 13g protein*

Fluffy Baked Eggs

Quick & Easy Tomato Soup, p. 66

CHAPTER TWO

SATISFYING
Soups &
Sandwiches

Easy Sloppy Joes, p. 74

Tomato Sandwiches, p. 56

Elaine Slabinski, Monroe Township, NJ

Creamy Asparagus Soup

This soup is so beautiful! Top with freshly steamed asparagus tips for the perfect garnish.

Makes 4 servings

1-1/2 lbs. asparagus trimmed, chopped and divided
14-1/2 oz. can low-sodium chicken broth
1 T. onion, minced
1/4 t. salt
1/4 t. white pepper
1/2 c. 2% milk

Set aside a few asparagus tips for garnish. Combine remaining ingredients except milk in a soup pot over medium heat. Bring to a boil; reduce heat and simmer 5 to 7 minutes, or until asparagus is tender. Working in small batches, ladle asparagus mixture into a blender. Add milk slowly and purée. Return mixture to soup pot and heat through without boiling. Steam or microwave reserved asparagus tips just until tender; use to garnish soup.

Nutrition Per Serving: *60 calories, 1g total fat, 1g sat fat, 4mg cholesterol, 213mg sodium, 9g carbohydrate, 4g fiber, 6g protein*

Kimberly Ascroft, Merritt Island, FL

Key West Burgers

Dress up a plain burger with slices of mango and fresh lime juice.

Serves 4

1 lb. lean ground beef
3 T. Key lime juice
1/4 c. fresh cilantro, chopped and divided
salt and pepper to taste
4 whole-wheat hamburger buns, split and toasted
1 mango, pitted, peeled and sliced
Optional: lettuce leaves

In a bowl, combine beef, lime juice, 3 tablespoons cilantro, salt and pepper. Form beef mixture into 4 patties. Spray a large skillet with non-stick vegetable spray. Cook patties over medium heat for 6 minutes. Flip patties, cover skillet and cook for another 6 minutes. Place lettuce on bottom halves of buns if using, and top with patties. Add Creamy Burger Spread onto bun tops. Top with mango slices and remaining chopped cilantro. Add bun tops.

CREAMY BURGER SPREAD:
1/2 c. light cream cheese, softened
1/2 c. plain Greek yogurt
3 green onion tops, chopped

Combine all ingredients until completely blended. Cover and refrigerate at least 15 minutes.

Nutrition Per Serving: *428 calories, 18g total fat, 8g sat fat, 90mg cholesterol, 446mg sodium, 37g carbohydrate, 5g fiber, 31g protein*

Key West Burgers

Crystal Bruns, Iliff, CO

Avocado Egg Salad Sandwiches

A fresh and delicious twist on egg salad...serve it with a hearty bread.

Makes 6 sandwiches

6 eggs, hard-boiled, peeled and
    chopped
2 avocados, halved, pitted and cubed
Optional: 1/4 c. red onion, minced
1/3 c. mayonnaise
1 T. mustard
salt and pepper to taste
12 slices bread

Mash eggs with a fork in a bowl until crumbly. Add remaining ingredients except bread slices. Gently mix together until blended. Spread egg mixture evenly over 6 bread slices. Top with remaining bread slices.

Nutrition Per Serving: *397 calories, 24g total fat, 4g sat fat, 217mg cholesterol, 491mg sodium, 35g carbohydrate, 5g fiber, 12g protein*

Rita Morgan, Pueblo, CO

Beef Bone Broth

This broth can be made in an electric pressure cooker or slow cooker.

Makes 1-1/2 quarts, serves 4

2 lbs. soup or oxtail bones
2 T. olive oil
1 medium onion, diced
2 carrots, chopped
2 stalks celery, chopped
1 clove garlic, pressed
1 t. salt
1 t. coarse pepper
6 c. water

Heat oven to 400 degrees. Place bones on baking sheet and roast for about 30 minutes, until browned. Remove from oven and set aside. *If using an electric pressure cooker*, select Sauté setting and add the oil, onion, carrots, celery and garlic. Sauté until softened, about 5 minutes. Place bones, salt, pepper and water in the electric pressure cooker. Secure the lid and set pressure release to Sealing. Select the Manual/Pressure setting and cook on high pressure for 60 minutes. After cooking time is up, use the Natural Release method to release pressure. Open the lid carefully; remove bones and vegetables and discard. Line a strainer with cheesecloth and set over a large bowl. Pour broth through the strainer and discard solids. *If using slow cooker*, in a skillet, sauté onion, carrots, celery and garlic in oil until softened, about 5 minutes. Place onion mixture, bones, salt, pepper and water in slow cooker. Cover and cook for 8 hours. Remove bones and vegetables; discard. Line a strainer with cheesecloth and set over a large bowl. Pour broth through the strainer and discard solids. *For both methods*, allow broth to cool; cover and refrigerate and use within 3 days, or freeze for up to 4 months. To use, skim and discard fat from surface of broth.

Nutrition Per Serving: *209 calories, 10g total fat, 4g sat fat, 56mg cholesterol, 488mg sodium, 0g carbohydrate, 0g fiber, 22g protein*

Beef Bone Broth

Jo Ann, Gooseberry Patch

Veggie Melts

This hearty vegetarian sandwich is one of our favorites! We use ciabatta bread, but French or Italian bread works well too.

Makes 4 servings

1 c. sliced baby portabella
   mushrooms
1/4 c. olive oil
1 loaf ciabatta bread, halved
   lengthwise
8-oz. jar whole roasted red peppers,
   drained
1-1/2 t. Italian seasoning
1 c. shredded Fontina cheese

In a skillet over medium heat, sauté mushrooms in olive oil until tender. Place bread halves on an ungreased baking sheet. On one bread half, layer peppers, mushrooms and Italian seasoning. Top both halves evenly with cheese. Broil until lightly golden. Assemble sandwich and cut into 4 pieces.

Nutrition Per Serving: *470 calories, 22g total fat, 7g sat fat, 31mg cholesterol, 938mg sodium, 52g carbohydrate, 2g fiber, 15g protein*

Allison May, Seattle, WA

Quick Chicken Salad Sandwich

I love chicken salad, but I don't have a lot of time to make it. This recipe is so easy and I can grill the chicken the night before.

Serves 4

2 trimmed chicken breasts, grilled,
   cooled and diced
1/2 c. celery, diced
1/2 c. light mayonnaise
1/2 t. salt
1/2 t. pepper
4 small brioche buns, split
Optional: sliced avocado, lettuce
   leaves

In a large bowl, mix the chicken, celery, mayonnaise, salt and pepper. Stir until well combined. Spread onto brioche buns; garnish with avocado and lettuce leaves, if desired.

Nutrition Per Serving: *354 calories, 20g total fat, 4g sat fat, 82mg cholesterol, 638mg sodium, 21g carbohydrate, 2g fiber, 21g protein*

Quick Chicken Salad Sandwich

Diana Duff, Cypress, CA

Chicken Chimies

My family loves this meal and requests it often. I have the chicken cooked the day before and have it ready to go in the refrigerator, so we can pull this meal together in a flash!

Serves 8

2 boneless, skinless chicken breasts, cooked and shredded
salt, pepper and garlic salt to taste
1 T. butter
10 8-inch flour tortillas
8-oz. pkg. shredded Monterey Jack cheese
6 green onions, diced
1 T. oil
Garnish: sour cream, guacamole, salsa
Optional: lettuce leaves

Sprinkle chicken with salt, pepper and garlic salt to taste. Melt butter in a large skillet over medium heat; add chicken and sauté about 3 minutes. Spoon chicken evenly onto tortillas. Top with cheese and green onions; fold sides up and roll up, burrito-style. Heat oil in a large skillet over medium-high heat. Add rolled-up tortillas and sauté 3 to 6 minutes, until golden. Serve with your choice of toppings and over lettuce leaves, if desired.

Nutrition Per Serving: *395 calories, 20g total fat, 8g sat fat, 57mg cholesterol, 507mg sodium, 33g carbohydrate, 1g fiber, 21g protein*

Amber Sutton, Naches, WA

Cherry Tomato Hummus Wraps

I love those little tomatoes that you can eat like candy straight from the vine...especially in a wrap!

Makes 4 servings

4 T. hummus
4 8-inch flour tortillas, warmed
1 c. cherry tomatoes, halved
1/2 c. Kalamata olives, chopped
1/3 c. crumbled feta cheese
6 sprigs fresh basil, snipped

Spread one tablespoon hummus down the center of each tortilla. Divide remaining ingredients evenly over hummus. To wrap up tortillas burrito-style, turn tortillas so that fillings are side-to-side. Fold in left and right sides of each tortilla; fold top and bottom edges over the filling.

Nutrition Per Serving: *223 calories, 9g total fat, 3g sat fat, 11mg cholesterol, 613mg sodium, 29g carbohydrate, 3g fiber, 7g protein*

GOOD TO KNOW
Even though a tomato is considered a fruit, it is not sugary as are many fruits. And even though the carbs in a tomato are simple carbs, they are still an excellent fruit choice to those on low-carb diets.

Cherry Tomato Hummus Wraps

Laura Seban, Saint Simons Island, GA

Egg Drop Ramen

Who says ramen noodles are just for college kids? This quick-to-make soup is perfect for any age. Once you try this, you'll make it over and over again!

Makes 2 to 3 servings

1-1/2 c. water
3-oz. pkg. chicken-flavored ramen noodles, uncooked and divided
2 eggs, beaten
2 slices American cheese, chopped
1/3 c. frozen peas, thawed

In a saucepan, bring water to a boil over medium heat. Add half of the seasoning packet, reserving the rest for another use. Stir in noodles; cook for 3 minutes. Add eggs, stirring quickly for 2 minutes to break them up. Add cheese and stir in well. Remove from heat; mix in peas and stir well. Serve in soup bowls.

Nutrition Per Serving: *207 calories, 8g total fat, 3g sat fat, 146mg cholesterol, 712mg sodium, 20g carbohydrate, 1g fiber, 11g protein*

Mary Jo Babiarz, Spring Grove, IL

Chili-Weather Chili

Serve with Italian bread and a plate of fresh fruit for a complete meal.

Serves 4

1 lb. ground beef
2 T. onion, diced
15-3/4 oz. can chili beans with chili sauce
16-oz. can tomato sauce
8-oz. jar salsa
Garnish: shredded cheese

Brown beef and onion together in a large stockpot; drain. Add remaining ingredients except garnish. Bring to a boil and reduce heat to medium; add 1/2 cup water if mixture is too thick. Cover and simmer for 30 minutes, stirring occasionally. Garnish with shredded cheese.

Nutrition Per Serving: *428 calories, 13g total fat, 5g sat fat, 73mg cholesterol, 1974mg sodium, 47g carbohydrate, 11g fiber, 35g protein*

GOOD TO KNOW
Beans are a thrifty way to get plenty of protein and fiber and you can eat them in so many yummy ways!

Chili-Weather Chili

Julie Horn, Christney, IN

Texas Steak Sandwiches

Everyone loves a good steak sandwich and this one fills the bill!

Serves 8

8 slices whole-grain bread
3/4 lb. cooked roast beef, sliced
1 T. steak sauce
4 slices provolone cheese, halved
1 green pepper, sliced and sautéed
Optional: 1 red onion, sliced and
    sautéed

Place bread on an ungreased baking sheet. Bake at 425 degrees for 5 minutes per side, or until slightly toasted. Warm roast beef in a skillet over medium heat until most of juice has evaporated; stir in steak sauce. Place one cheese piece on each toast slice. Divide beef evenly among toast slices; top with remaining cheese pieces and sautéed green pepper and onion slices, if using. Place beef-topped toast on an ungreased baking sheet; bake at 425 degrees until cheese melts.

Nutrition Per Serving: *212 calories, 7g total fat, 4g sat fat, 51mg cholesterol, 265mg sodium, 14g carbohydrate, 3g fiber, 22g protein*

Carol Smith, West Lawn, PA

Honey-Barbecued Pork

I like to get this started in my slow cooker before I go to work. When we all get home we have a great meal waiting for us!

Makes 8 servings

3-lb. pork roast
1 onion, chopped
12-oz. bottle low-sodium barbecue
    sauce
1/4 c. honey
8 sandwich rolls, split

Place pork in a slow cooker. Add onion, barbecue sauce and honey. Cover and cook on low setting for 6 to 8 hours. Shred or chop pork and serve on rolls.

Nutrition Per Serving: *479 calories, 13g total fat, 4g sat fat, 94mg cholesterol, 339mg sodium, 46g carbohydrate, 1g fiber, 41g protein*

Honey-Barbecued Pork

Elisa Thompson, Celina, TN

Mini Ham & Cheesewiches

I always take these little sandwiches to family gatherings. I have a very large family, so I have to fix lots!

Makes one dozen

17-oz. pkg. brown & serve dinner
    rolls
8-oz. pkg. sliced deli ham
12 slices American cheese
Garnish: melted butter, garlic salt

Slice each roll in half like a hamburger bun. Folding to fit, place a slice of ham and a slice of cheese on each roll bottom. Add tops; brush with butter and sprinkle with garlic salt. Arrange on an ungreased baking sheet. Bake at 450 degrees until golden and cheese is melted.

Nutrition Per Serving: *180 calories, 5g total fat, 2g sat fat, 18mg cholesterol, 729mg sodium, 22g carbohydrate, 1g fiber, 12g protein*

Wanda Leuty, Swansen, IL

Wanda's Wimpies

This is an easy Sloppy Joe recipe for busy parents and grandparents.

Makes 8 servings

1-1/2 lbs. lean ground beef
salt and pepper to taste
10-3/4 oz. can tomato soup
1/2 c. tangy-flavored low-sodium
    catsup
8 sandwich buns

Brown beef in a heavy saucepan; add salt and pepper to taste. Add soup and catsup; reduce heat and simmer until thick. Spoon onto buns to serve.

Nutrition Per Serving: *305 calories, 11g total fat, 4g sat fat, 55mg cholesterol, 473mg sodium, 30g carbohydrate, 1g fiber, 22g protein*

Diane Long, Delaware, OH

Tomato Sandwiches

Use garden tomatoes warm from the summer sun to make these sandwiches extra special.

Makes 5 servings

10 slices pumpernickel bread
3 tomatoes, thickly sliced
10 sprigs watercress
1 red onion, sliced
1 green pepper, sliced
1/4 t. pepper
Optional: 1 T. mayonnaise

Top each of 5 bread slices with tomato slices, 2 sprigs of watercress, a slice of onion and 2 slices of green pepper. Sprinkle with salt and pepper. Spread mayonnaise, if using, over remaining bread slices and top sandwiches.

Nutrition Per Serving: *170 calories, 4g total fat, 1g sat fat, 1mg cholesterol, 332mg sodium, 29g carbohydrate, 5g fiber, 6g protein*

Tomato Sandwiches

Deborah Neuman, San Felipe, TX

Texas Ranch Soup

This soup is super fast to make. Using canned vegetables makes it easy, and the taco seasoning mix adds so much yummy flavor.

Serves 6

1-1/2 lbs. ground beef, browned and
    drained
2 15-oz. cans ranch-style beans
2 15-oz. cans no-salt corn
2 14-1/2 oz. cans diced tomatoes
1-1/4 oz. pkg. taco seasoning mix
Garnish: crushed tortilla chips,
    shredded Cheddar cheese

Combine all ingredients except garnish in a large stockpot; bring to a boil. Reduce heat and simmer for 15 minutes. Spoon into serving bowls; garnish with crushed tortilla chips and shredded Cheddar cheese.

Nutrition Per Serving: *457 calories, 14g total fat, 5g sat fat, 73mg cholesterol, 1512mg sodium, 54g carbohydrate, 11g fiber, 33g protein*

Bev Fisher, Mesa, AZ

Grilled Havarti

Now that my children are grown, I'm always looking for recipes that call for ingredients they wouldn't eat. This sandwich is so tasty, I wanted another one the next day after I first tried it!

Makes 4 sandwiches

8 slices French bread
2 t. butter, softened and divided
4 T. apricot preserves
1/4 lb. Havarti cheese, sliced
1 avocado, halved, pitted and sliced

Spread 4 slices bread on one side with half the butter and all the preserves. Top with cheese, avocado and another slice of bread; spread remaining butter on outside of sandwiches. Heat a large skillet over medium heat. Cook sandwiches for 2 to 3 minutes, until bread is golden and cheese begins to melt. Turn over; press down slightly with a spatula. Cook until golden.

Nutrition Per Serving: *595 calories, 18g total fat, 8g sat fat, 32mg cholesterol, 1019mg sodium, 88g carbohydrate, 5g fiber, 22g protein*

Michelle McFadden-DiNicola,
Highland Park, NJ

Grandma's Pastina

The tiny pasta in this soup makes it so special and fun for the entire family! We looked forward to this lunch with Grandma on the weekends.

Makes 2 to 3 servings

4 c. water
3 cubes chicken bouillon
2 cubes beef bouillon
3/4 c. tiny star or alphabet soup
    pasta, uncooked
1/2 c. fresh parsley, coarsely chopped
1/8 t. pepper
2 eggs
salt and pepper to taste
Optional: grated Parmesan cheese

Place water and bouillon cubes in a soup pot over medium heat. Stir to break up bouillon cubes once the water is simmering. Stir in pasta, parsley and pepper; boil until pasta is tender, 3 to 4 minutes. Turn heat down to lowest possible setting. In a small bowl, whisk eggs lightly with a fork; season with salt and pepper to taste. While stirring the soup, slowly pour in eggs. Continue stirring until eggs begin to turn white. Allow eggs to cook through, about one additional minute. Sprinkle with Parmesan cheese, if desired. Serve hot.

Nutrition Per Serving: *197 calories, 5g total fat, 1g sat fat, 142mg cholesterol, 1194mg sodium, 28g carbohydrate, 1g fiber, 10g protein*

Deborah Lomax, Peoria, IL

Raspberry-Dijon Baguettes

Pair grilled chicken breasts with a tangy-sweet sauce on French bread...a masterpiece!

Serves 4

1 baguette, cut into 4 pieces
1 T. Dijon mustard
2 T. raspberry jam
4 boneless, skinless chicken breasts, grilled and sliced
2 c. arugula leaves
Optional: red onion slices

Slice the baguette pieces. Spread one side with mustard. Spread remaining slices with raspberry jam. Arrange a layer of grilled chicken over mustard; top with arugula and onion, if desired. Cover with remaining baguette slices.

Nutrition Per Serving: *504 calories, 17g total fat, 5g sat fat, 108mg cholesterol, 564mg sodium, 44g carbohydrate, 2g fiber, 43g protein*

Raspberry-Dijon Baguettes

Jennifer Inacio, Hummelstown, PA

Jen's Pulled Pork

There's no right or wrong amount of sauce to use...simply stir in as much as you'd like. You can also add sliced jalapeños, minced garlic or sautéed onions and green peppers.

Serves 10

3 to 4-lb. boneless pork loin roast, halved
2-ltr. bottle cola
28-oz. bottle honey barbecue sauce
10 hamburger buns, split

Place roast in a 5-quart slow cooker; add cola. Cover and cook on high setting one hour; reduce heat to low setting and cook, fat-side up, 10 to 12 more hours. Remove from slow cooker; remove and discard any fat. Discard cooking liquids; clean and wipe slow cooker with a paper towel. Shred pork and return to slow cooker; add barbecue sauce to taste. Cover and cook on low setting one more hour, or until heated through. Add more sauce, if desired. Serve on buns.

Nutrition Per Serving: *560 calories, 22g total fat, 7g sat fat, 87mg cholesterol, 1147mg sodium, 54g carbohydrate, 1g fiber, 33g protein*

Judy Bailey, Des Moines, IA

Homemade Chicken Broth

Make this broth in your electric pressure cooker or slow cooker. Either way, it is delicious!

Makes 1-1/2 quarts, serves 6

3 lbs. chicken parts (such as wings, backs, legs)
3 carrots, peeled and cut into 2-inch pieces
2 stalks celery, cut into 2-inch pieces
1 T. fresh chives, chopped
4 sprigs fresh parsley
1 t. salt
1 t. pepper
6 c. water

If using electric pressure cooker, combine all ingredients in pot. Secure lid and set pressure release to Sealing. Select Manual/Pressure Cook and cook at high pressure for 40 minutes. Once cooking is complete, release pressure by using Natural Release method. Strain broth through colander into a large bowl; discard bones and solids. *If using slow cooker,* combine all ingredients in cooker. Cook on high for 6 hours. Strain broth through colander into a large bowl; discard bones and solids. *For both methods,* cover and refrigerate to use within 3 days, or freeze for up to 4 months. To use, skim and discard fat from surface of broth.

Nutrition Per Serving: *45 calories, 1g total fat, 0g sat fat, 25mg cholesterol, 388mg sodium, 3g carbohydrate, 0g fiber, 6g protein*

Homemade Chicken Broth

Paulette Cunningham, Lompoc, CA

Too-Simple Tortilla Soup

Top this soup with a couple of slices of avocado, fresh cilantro or a dollop of sour cream.

Serves 8

2 10-oz. cans chicken, drained
2 14-1/2 oz. cans low-sodium
  chicken broth
2 15-oz. cans white hominy, drained
16-oz. jar salsa
1 T. cumin

Combine all ingredients in a stockpot; bring to a boil. Reduce heat, and warm through.

Nutrition Per Serving: *244 calories, 8g total fat, 2g sat fat, 35mg cholesterol, 587mg sodium, 21g carbohydrate, 4g fiber, 22g protein*

Jill Valentine, Jackson, TN

Slow-Cooker Butternut Squash Soup

Just chop a few ingredients and combine in the slow cooker for a delicious gourmet soup....so easy!

Serves 8

2-1/2 lbs. butternut squash, peeled,
  halved, seeded and cubed
2 c. leeks, chopped
2 Granny Smith apples, peeled,
  cored and diced
2 14-1/2 oz. cans chicken broth
1 c. water
seasoned salt and white pepper to
  taste
Garnish: freshly ground nutmeg and
  sour cream

Combine squash, leeks, apples, broth and water in a 4-quart slow cooker. Cover and cook on high setting for 4 hours or until squash and leeks are tender. Carefully purée the hot soup in 3 or 4 batches in a food processor or blender until smooth. Add seasoned salt and white pepper. Garnish with nutmeg and sour cream.

Nutrition Per Serving: *112 calories, 1g total fat, 0g sat fat, 2mg cholesterol, 41mg sodium, 26g carbohydrate, 4g fiber, 4g protein*

Slow-Cooker Butternut Squash Soup

Janie Reed, Zanesville, OH

Toasted Green Tomato Sandwiches

Heat up your skillet to make this hot, buttery favorite.

Serves 4

1-1/2 to 2 c. cornmeal
salt and pepper to taste
2 green tomatoes, sliced 1/4-inch thick
oil or shortening for frying
2 to 3 T. butter, softened
8 slices whole-wheat bread
Optional: basil mayonnaise, curly leaf lettuce

Combine cornmeal and seasonings in a large plastic zipping bag. Shake to mix well. Add tomato slices, and gently shake to coat. Remove tomatoes from bag, shaking off excess cornmeal mixture. Heat oil or shortening in a large skillet over medium heat; fry tomatoes until golden on both sides. Remove from skillet. Spread butter on one side of each bread slice. Arrange 4 slices, butter-side down, in skillet. Cook over medium heat until toasted. Repeat with remaining bread slices. Spread mayonnaise over untoasted sides of bread, if desired. Top with tomatoes and lettuce, if desired. Close sandwich with another slice of bread. Cook sandwiches over medium heat, turning once, until golden on both sides.

Nutrition Per Serving: *433 calories, 14g total fat, 7g sat fat, 26mg cholesterol, 246mg sodium, 67g carbohydrate, 8g fiber, 12g protein*

Gretchen Ham, Pine City, NY

Quick & Easy Tomato Soup

Fresh basil really makes this soup special. The flavors get even better when it is warmed up the next day!

Makes 10 servings

1/4 c. butter, sliced
1 c. fresh basil, chopped
2 28-oz. cans crushed tomatoes
2 cloves garlic, minced
1 qt. whole milk
salt and pepper to taste
Garnish: fresh parsley, fresh chives, croutons

In a large saucepan, melt butter over medium heat. Add basil; sauté for 2 minutes. Add tomatoes with juice and garlic; reduce heat and simmer for 20 minutes. Remove from heat; let cool slightly. Working in batches, transfer tomato mixture to a blender and purée. Strain into a separate saucepan and add milk, mixing very well. Reheat soup over medium-low heat; add salt and pepper to taste. Garnish as desired.

Nutrition Per Serving: *150 calories, 8g total fat, 5g sat fat, 22mg cholesterol, 247mg sodium, 17g carbohydrate, 3g fiber, 6g protein*

Quick & Easy Tomato Soup

Janice Woods, Northern Cambria, PA

Chilled Melon Soup

So refreshing on a warm summer day.

Makes 6 servings

3 c. cantaloupe melon, peeled, seeded
   and chopped
1/4 c. orange juice, divided
1/4 t. salt, divided
3 c. honeydew melon, peeled, seeded
   and chopped
Garnish: fresh mint sprigs or orange
   slices

In a blender, process cantaloupe, half the juice and half the salt until smooth. Cover and refrigerate. Repeat with honeydew and remaining ingredients except garnish. Refrigerate, covered, in separate containers. To serve, pour equal amounts of each mixture at the same time on opposite sides of individual soup bowls. Garnish as desired.

Nutrition Per Serving: *62 calories, 0g total fat, 0g sat fat, 0mg cholesterol, 152mg sodium, 16g carbohydrate, 1g fiber, 1g protein*

Marilyn Meyers Orange City, FL

Callie Coe's Chicken & Dumplings

This Southern favorite is the ultimate comfort food. Like biscuit dough, the less the dumpling dough is handled, the lighter and more tender it will be.

Serves 6

3 to 4 lbs. bone-in chicken, cut up
3 qts. water
salt and pepper to taste
4 eggs, hard-boiled, peeled and
   chopped

Place chicken pieces in a large pan; add water, salt and pepper. Bring to a boil; reduce heat and simmer until tender and juices run clear when chicken is pierced with a fork, about one hour. Remove chicken, reserving broth in pan. Let chicken cool; remove meat, discarding bones, and return meat to chicken broth. Add chopped eggs. Bring broth to a boil and add Dumplings one batch at a time; stir well before adding each new batch. After adding last batch, cover and simmer until tender, about 20 minutes. Remove from heat; let stand a few minutes before serving.

DUMPLINGS:
4 c. self-rising flour
1 to 1-1/4 c. warm water

Mix flour with enough water to make a dough that can be rolled out. Divide dough into 4 batches. Roll out each batch of dough 1/2-inch thick on a lightly floured surface; cut into strips.

Nutrition Per Serving: *486 calories, 10g total fat, 3g sat fat, 202mg cholesterol, 922mg sodium, 62g carbohydrate, 2g fiber, 33g protein*

Callie Coe's Chicken & Dumplings

Kathie Jester, Yadkinville, NC

Santa Fe Spicy Chicken Soup

With only 5 ingredients, this is a winner!

Serves 4

1 boneless, skinless chicken breast, cubed
2 to 3 potatoes, peeled and cubed
14-1/2 oz. can diced tomatoes with green chiles
14-oz. can chicken broth
1-1/4 oz. pkg. taco seasoning mix

Combine all ingredients in an ungreased microwave-safe one-quart casserole dish. Mix well; cover tightly with plastic wrap. Microwave on high for 13 to 16 minutes, until chicken is cooked and potatoes are tender. Let stand for 2 minutes before removing from microwave. Remove plastic wrap carefully.

Nutrition Per Serving: *171 calories, 1g total fat, 0g sat fat, 16mg cholesterol, 903mg sodium, 31g carbohydrate, 4g fiber, 11g protein*

Christine Gordon, Rapid City, SD

French Bread Pizza Burgers

A quick & easy dinner! The kids will love to help Mom make these yummy sandwiches.

Serves 6 to 8

1 loaf French bread, halved lengthwise
15-oz. can pizza sauce
1 lb. ground pork sausage, browned and drained
3-1/2-oz. pkg. sliced pepperoni
8-oz. pkg. shredded mozzarella cheese

Place both halves of loaf on an ungreased baking sheet, cut sides up. Spread with pizza sauce; top with sausage, pepperoni and cheese. Bake at 350 degrees for 15 minutes, or until cheese is melted. Slice to serve.

Nutrition Per Serving: *493 calories, 26g total fat, 10g sat fat, 73mg cholesterol, 1101mg sodium, 37g carbohydrate, 2g fiber, 26g protein*

KITCHEN TIP
Fill a big shaker with a favorite all-purpose spice mixture...keep it by the stove for a dash of flavor on soups, meats and veggies as they cook.

French Bread Pizza Burgers

Audrey Lett, Newark, DE

Suzanne's Tomato Melt

I love this as a quick dinner with a fresh salad...it is so easy to make!

Makes one serving

1/4 c. shredded Cheddar cheese
1 onion bagel or English muffin, split
2 tomato slices
1 T. Parmesan cheese
fresh basil leaves

Sprinkle half the Cheddar cheese over each bagel or English muffin half. Top with a tomato slice. Sprinkle half the Parmesan cheese over each tomato. Add fresh basil leaf on top. Broil about 6 inches from heat for 4 to 5 minutes, or until cheese is bubbly.

Nutrition Per Serving: *276 calories, 12g total fat, 7g sat fat, 33mg cholesterol, 527mg sodium, 28g carbohydrate, 2g fiber, 14g protein*

Janae Mallonee, Marlboro, MA

Caboosta Cabbage Soup

Our family loves this rich pork soup on a cold winter night.

Serves 4

6 c. water
28-oz. can crushed tomatoes
1/2 to 2/3 head cabbage, shredded
1-1/2 c. boneless pork, diced
1 bay leaf
salt and pepper to taste

In a soup pot over medium heat, combine water, tomatoes with juice, cabbage, pork and bay leaf. Bring to a boil; reduce heat to low. Simmer for about 30 minutes, stirring occasionally, until pork is cooked and cabbage is tender. At serving time, discard bay leaf; season with salt and pepper.

Nutrition Per Serving: *387 calories, 16g total fat, 5g sat fat, 120mg cholesterol, 357mg sodium, 15g carbohydrate, 4g fiber, 47g protein*

KITCHEN TIP
Purchase shredded cabbage in the salad aisle of your grocery store and use it in salads and soups. It works great and saves the shredding time.

Caboosta Cabbage Soup

Gladys Kielar, Whitehouse, OH

Creamy Cucumber Soup

English, or hothouse, cucumbers have thin skins, few seeds, and a mild flavor.

Makes 8 servings

3/4 c. chicken broth
3 green onions
2 T. white vinegar
1/2 t. salt
1/4 t. pepper
2-1/2 lbs. English cucumbers (about 3 large), peeled, seeded, chopped and divided
3 c. Greek yogurt
Garnish: toasted slivered almonds, additional pepper and chopped red pepper

Process chicken broth, green onions, vinegar, salt, pepper and half of chopped cucumbers in a food processor or blender until smooth, stopping to scrape down sides. Add yogurt and pulse until blended. Pour into a large bowl; stir in remaining chopped cucumbers. Cover and chill 4 to 24 hours. Garnish as desired.

Nutrition Per Serving: *73 calories, 1g total fat, 0g sat fat, 2mg cholesterol, 226mg sodium, 11g carbohydrate, 1g fiber, 7g protein*

Lizzy Burnley, Ankeny, IA

Easy Sloppy Joes

Instant brown rice is the secret to making this Sloppy Joe easy to make and a little bit healthier.

Serves 6

1-1/2 lbs. ground beef
1 T. low-sodium beef bouillon granules
1/2 c. instant brown rice, uncooked
1/4 c. catsup
1/2 c. water
salt and pepper to taste
6 hamburger buns, split

Brown beef in a skillet until all the pink in beef is gone. Drain and return to skillet. Add remaining ingredients except buns and bring to a boil. Boil for one minute. Remove from heat and cover for 10 minutes. Serve on hamburger buns.

Nutrition Per Serving: *356 calories, 13g total fat, 5g sat fat, 73mg cholesterol, 384mg sodium, 30g carbohydrate, 1g fiber, 27g protein*

Easy Sloppy Joes

Pork & Peach Kabobs, p. 96

CHAPTER THREE

GOOD-FOR-YOU
Grilling

Simply-Grilled Peaches, p. 108

Crunchy Chicken Sandwich, p. 78

Jo Ann, Gooseberry Patch

Ginger-Lime Grilled Salmon

Serve this delicious dish with a spinach salad made using sliced tomatoes and cucumbers for a complete meal.

Serves 4 to 6

2 T. butter, melted
2 T. fresh ginger, peeled and minced
2 T. lime zest
1 T. lime juice
1/2 t. salt
1/2 t. pepper
2 lbs. salmon fillets, 1-inch thick
Garnish: lime wedges

In a small bowl, combine all ingredients except salmon and garnish. Rub mixture over salmon fillets. Place fish on a lightly oiled grate over medium-high heat. Cover and grill salmon about 5 minutes on each side, until fish flakes easily with a fork. Garnish with lime wedges.

Nutrition Per Serving: *347 calories, 24g total fat, 7g sat fat, 92mg cholesterol, 283mg sodium, 1g carbohydrate, 0g fiber, 3g protein*

Sonna Johnson, Goldfield, IA

Crunchy Chicken Sandwich

The barbecue sauce in these sandwiches gives it just the right sweetness and tang.

Serves 6

1 lb. ground chicken
1/4 c. low-sodium honey barbecue sauce
3/4 c. mini shredded wheat cereal or corn cereal, crushed
1 egg, beaten
1/8 t. salt
1/8 t. pepper
6 hamburger whole-grain buns, split
Garnish: tomato and onion slices, lettuce leaves

Mix all ingredients together except buns; form into 6 patties. Grill for 5 to 6 minutes per side, until no longer pink in the center. Serve on buns, garnished as desired.

Nutrition Per Serving: *270 calories, 9g total fat, 2g sat fat, 99mg cholesterol, 391mg sodium, 29g carbohydrate, 4g fiber, 21g protein*

KITCHEN TIP
Crush a boxful of cereal all at once and store the crumbs in a canister to have on hand for recipes that call for them.

Crunchy Chicken Sandwich

Lori Rosenberg, Cleveland, OH

Grilled Pepperoni Log

This recipe is a real crowd-pleaser! Pepperoni Logs on the grill have a wonderful smoky taste and are easy to make and to clean up.

Makes 14 servings

16-oz. loaf frozen bread dough, thawed
4-oz. pkg. sliced pepperoni
1 c. shredded mozzarella cheese
1/4 c. grated Parmesan cheese
1-1/2 t. Italian seasoning

Preheat grill until hot, about 375 degrees. On a lightly floured surface, roll out thawed bread dough into a 13-inch by 9-inch rectangle. Arrange pepperoni and cheeses evenly over dough. Sprinkle with seasoning. Roll up dough jelly-roll style, starting on one long edge; pinch seam to seal. Place dough seam-side down on grate over indirect heat. Cook for 20 minutes on each side. Slice to serve.

Nutrition Per Serving: *160 calories, 6g total fat, 3g sat fat, 15mg cholesterol, 417mg sodium, 18g carbohydrate, 1g fiber, 8g protein*

Sharon Demers, Dolores, CO

Firecracker Grilled Salmon

We love making this spicy salmon on the grill and serve it with fresh green beans and quinoa. It is a favorite summer meal.

Makes 4 servings

4 4-oz. salmon fillets
3 T. Italian dressing
2 T. green onions, chopped
1 clove garlic, minced
1/2 t. red pepper flakes
1/4 t. salt

Place salmon in a casserole dish. Whisk together remaining ingredients and pour over salmon. Cover with plastic wrap; refrigerate 4 to 6 hours. Remove salmon, discarding marinade. Place on an aluminum foil-lined grill that has been sprayed with non-stick vegetable spray. Grill 10 minutes per inch of thickness, measured at thickest part, until fish flakes easily with a fork. Turn halfway through cooking.

Nutrition Per Serving: *265 calories, 18g total fat, 4g sat fat, 62mg cholesterol, 391mg sodium, 1g carbohydrate, 0g fiber, 23g protein*

Firecracker Grilled Salmon

Liz Lanza Brownsville, PA

Grilled London Broil

My family has been enjoying this luscious steak for years. It's so easy to prepare, and the simple marinade is delicious.

Serves 10

3 to 4-lb. beef flank steak
1/3 c. soy sauce
2/3 c. teriyaki sauce

Place steak in a glass casserole dish. Mix together sauces in a small bowl; pour over steak. Cover and refrigerate 8 hours to overnight, turning occasionally. Drain, discarding marinade. Grill steak over high heat to desired doneness, about 4 to 5 minutes on each side for medium. Remove steak from grill; let stand for 10 minutes. Slice steak thinly across the grain.

Nutrition Per Serving: *247 calories, 11g total fat, 5g sat fat, 55mg cholesterol, 253mg sodium, 1g carbohydrate, 0g fiber, 34g protein*

Jo Ann, Gooseberry Patch

Citrus-Grilled Pork Tenderloin

These little medallions of tenderloin are so tasty with the sweet orange marmalade marinade. We like them with grilled potatoes.

Serves 4

1 lb. pork tenderloin, sliced 3/4-inch thick
1/2 t. pepper
1/3 c. orange marmalade
1/4 c. fresh mint, chopped
1/4 c. low-sodium soy sauce
1 clove garlic, minced

Sprinkle pork slices with pepper. Combine remaining ingredients; stir well. Brush over pork, reserving remaining marmalade mixture. Place pork on a lightly greased grill over high heat; grill for 3 minutes per side, or until no longer pink. Baste frequently with reserved marmalade mixture. Place marmalade mixture in a saucepan and bring to a boil over medium heat; cook for one minute. Drizzle over pork.

Nutrition Per Serving: *197 calories, 3g total fat, 1g sat fat, 73mg cholesterol, 606mg sodium, 19g carbohydrate, 0g fiber, 24g protein*

Citrus-Grilled Pork Tenderloin

Diane Brulc, Brookfield, WI

Evelyn's Grilled Pork Loin

My mom made this for our family get-togethers to serve with all our favorite sides. We always played a game outdoors before dinner. Such fond memories!

Serves 8

3-lb. boneless pork loin roast
1 c. low-sodium soy sauce
1/2 c. sherry or apple juice
1 t. mustard
1 t. ground ginger
1/2 t. salt

Place roast in a shallow glass dish. Combine remaining ingredients in a bowl and pour over roast. Cover and refrigerate for 2 hours to overnight. Drain marinade into a small saucepan; bring to a boil for about 3 minutes. Place roast on a grate over medium-high heat, 6 to 8 inches above heat. Grill, covered, for 1-1/2 to 2 hours, turning and brushing with marinade every 30 minutes. Slice roast thinly to serve.

Nutrition Per Serving: *276 calories, 11g total fat, 4g sat fat, 94mg cholesterol, 970mg sodium, 3g carbohydrate, 0g fiber, 38g protein*

Amy Thomason Hunt, Traphill, NC

Balsamic Grilled Tomatoes

These tomatoes are a wonderful side dish for grilled steak. They're tasty and look so pretty on the plate, yet are easy to do.

Serves 4

4 tomatoes, halved
1/4 c. balsamic vinaigrette salad dressing
1/4 c. grated Parmesan cheese
Optional: fresh basil

Place tomatoes in a disposable 13"x9" aluminum foil baking pan, cut-side up. Drizzle with salad dressing; sprinkle with cheese and basil if using. Place pan on a grate over medium heat. Cook for 15 minutes, or until tomatoes are soft and cheese is golden.

Nutrition Per Serving: *119 calories, 9g total fat, 1g sat fat, 6mg cholesterol, 232mg sodium, 7g carbohydrate, 2g fiber, 3g protein*

GOOD TO KNOW
Heirloom tomatoes usually have more flavor and are juicier than common variety hybrids. They also add beautiful color to any dish.

Balsamic Grilled Tomatoes

Emily Martin, Ontario, Canada

Fish-Ka-Bobs

Whether you choose salmon or halibut, these fish-ka-bobs will become a favorite grilling dish for your family.

Makes 6 servings

1-1/2 lbs. salmon or halibut fillets, sliced into 1-1/2 inch thick strips
4 to 6 skewers, soaked in water
1 c. olive oil & vinegar salad dressing
2 T. lemon juice
1/4 c. fresh Italian parsley, chopped
1 T. fresh rosemary, chopped

If using salmon, remove and discard skin. Thread fish strips onto skewers. Place skewers in a shallow glass dish. Whisk together remaining ingredients in a bowl; drizzle over fish. Cover and refrigerate 30 minutes, turning skewers occasionally. Drain, discarding marinade. Place skewers on a lightly oiled grill over high heat. Cover and cook for 4 minutes per side, or until fish flakes easily with a fork.

Nutrition Per Serving: *306 calories, 22g total fat, 3g sat fat, 62mg cholesterol, 198mg sodium, 3g carbohydrate, 0g fiber, 23g protein*

Kim Henry, Library, PA

Dad's Favorite Grilled Potatoes

You can use any potatoes you like in this recipe...we like redskin potatoes the best.

Serves 8

4 to 5 potatoes, sliced
1 onion, sliced
1 to 2 green peppers, sliced
salt and pepper to taste
1/4 c. butter, sliced
salad seasoning to taste

Combine potatoes, onion and green peppers in a grill-safe pan; sprinkle with salt and pepper to taste. Sprinkle with butter slices and salad seasoning. Grill until tender.

Nutrition Per Serving: *163 calories, 6g total fat, 4g sat fat, 15mg cholesterol, 10mg sodium, 27g carbohydrate, 4g fiber, 3g protein*

GOOD TO KNOW
Whether you prefer redskiin potatoes, Yukon Gold or russets, humble potatoes pack a great deal of nutrition. They are high in potassium and vitamin C.

Dad's Favorite Grilled Potatoes

Emma Brown, Saskatchewan, Canada

Maple Pork Chops

The sweetness of the maple syrup and saltiness of the soy sauce go so well together. My family can't get enough of these...I usually have to double the recipe!

Makes 4 servings

1/4 c. maple syrup
3 T. soy sauce
1 clove garlic, minced
4 pork chops

In a bowl, whisk together syrup, soy sauce and garlic; reserve 1/4 cup of mixture. Add pork chops to remaining mixture in bowl. Cover and refrigerate for at least 15 minutes to overnight. Drain, discarding mixture in bowl. Grill over medium-high heat until browned and cooked through, about 6 minutes per side. Drizzle pork chops with reserved syrup mixture before serving.

Nutrition Per Serving: *255 calories, 7g total fat, 2g sat fat, 123mg cholesterol, 304mg sodium, 7g carbohydrate, 0g fiber, 40g protein*

KITCHEN TIP
Have a squirt bottle of water handy when you are grilling to keep skewers or husks moist and to prevent burning.

Henry Burnley, Ankeny, IA

Grilled Iowa Corn

No matter how you eat it, Iowa sweet corn is the best. We like to grill it in the husk and then season it differently every time!

Serves 4

4 ears sweet corn in the husk
1 T. olive oil
1/2 t. salt
1/2 t. pepper
1 T. butter
3 T. chopped basil
Optional: 1/2 t. smoked paprika

Prepare the corn by carefully pulling back the husks and removing any silks. Gently pull the husks back up over the corn. Fill a large plastic bag with water and place the corn in the water to soak. (This will prevent the husks from burning while grilling.) Keep the corn in the refrigerator in the water for a least one hour or overnight. Remove the corn from the water and pull back the husks. Brush with olive oil and sprinkle with salt and pepper. Place on a medium-hot grill and grill until tender, about 5 to 10 minutes, being careful not to burn the husks. Remove from heat and spread with butter and basil. Sprinkle with smoked paprika, if desired.

Nutrition Per Serving: *177 calories, 7g total fat, 2g sat fat, 8mg cholesterol, 297mg sodium, 30g carbohydrate, 4g fiber, 4g protein*

Grilled Iowa Corn

Barb Bargdill, Gooseberry Patch

Grilled Italiano Spread

This is such an easy appetizer to prepare at a cookout!

Serves 12

8-oz. pkg. Neufchâtel cheese
1/4 c. basil pesto sauce
1 roma tomato, chopped
1/4 c. finely shredded Italian-blend cheese
shredded wheat crackers

Unwrap Neufchâtel cheese and place on a piece of heavy-duty foil. Top with pesto, tomato and shredded cheese. Place foil on grate over medium heat. Cover and grill for 8 to 10 minutes, until shredded cheese is melted and Neufchâtel cheese is softened but still holds its shape. Serve warm with crackers.

Nutrition Per Serving: *78 calories, 7g total fat, 3g sat fat, 16mg cholesterol, 120mg sodium, 1g carbohydrate, 0g fiber, 3g protein*

Delores Begansky, Wilmington, CT

Garlic & Mustard Burgers

No one will be able to resist these tasty grilled burgers!

Serves 4

1 lb. ground beef
3 T. country-style Dijon mustard
4 cloves garlic, chopped
4 Monterey Jack cheese slices
Optional: 7-oz. jar roasted red peppers, drained
4 hamburger buns, split and toasted

Mix together beef, mustard and garlic. Shape mixture into 4 patties about 3/4-inch thick. Cover and grill patties for 12 to 15 minutes, to desired doneness. Top with cheese and peppers, if desired. Serve on toasted buns.

Nutrition Per Serving: *422 calories, 20g total fat, 9g sat fat, 95mg cholesterol, 1255mg sodium, 25g carbohydrate, 2g fiber, 34g protein*

Garlic & Mustard Burgers

Brenda Schlosser, Brighton, CO

Pesto-Brie Grilled Chicken

A dish I came up with just for the love of basil and Brie together. Serve with pasta tossed with olive oil, sun-dried tomatoes and fresh garlic...wonderful!

Serves 4

4 boneless, skinless chicken breasts
1/4 c. basil pesto sauce
4 slices Brie cheese, 1/4-inch thick
salt and pepper to taste

Place chicken on an oiled grate over medium-high heat. Grill for 3 to 5 minutes; turn chicken over. Spread each piece with one tablespoon pesto and top with a cheese slice. Cover; continue cooking for 3 to 5 minutes, until cheese is melted and chicken juices run clear.

Nutrition Per Serving: *281 calories, 16g total fat, 5g sat fat, 83mg cholesterol, 366mg sodium, 1g carbohydrate, 0g fiber, 30g protein*

Elijah Dahlstrom, Ames, IA

Grilled Brussels Sprouts

Grilling Brussels sprouts gives them a nice charred flavor and the bacon adds just the right salty crunchiness!

Serves 4

16 fresh Brussels sprouts, trimmed
1 T. olive oil
1 t. lemon zest
1/2 t. salt
1/2 t. pepper
1/2 c. bacon, crisply cooked and crumbled

Make a small slit in the end of each Brussels sprout. Place the sprouts in a microwave-safe bowl and add one cup of water. Microwave for 2 minutes; drain. In a large bowl, mix oil, lemon zest, salt and pepper. Add the spouts; stir. When sprouts are nicely coated, place on oiled grill grates on medium-high heat, turning every 2 to 3 minutes, cooking until charred, about 10 minutes. Remove from grill and garnish with bacon.

Nutrition Per Serving: *104 calories, 7g total fat, 2g sat fat, 9mg cholesterol, 498mg sodium, 7g carbohydrate, 3g fiber, 6g protein*

Grilled Brussels Sprouts

Ashley Compoli, Ontario, Canada

Tom's BBQ Ribs

My husband Tom is the BBQ chef at our house. He always fixes ribs this way, and they are wonderful!

Makes 6 servings

2 T. chili powder
1 T. paprika
1 T. pepper
1 t. cayenne pepper
5 lbs. pork back ribs
brown sugar barbecue sauce to taste

Combine all spices in a small bowl. Coat ribs with spice mixture on both sides; wrap ribs in a double thickness of aluminum foil. Bake at 350 degrees for about 20 minutes. Preheat grill on high; remove ribs from oven and turn grill down to medium. Place ribs, still wrapped in foil, on grate. Cook for about one hour, turning occasionally, until tender. Remove ribs from grill. Increase grill to high heat; brush grill lightly with oil. Unwrap ribs and place on grate; brush with barbecue sauce. Cover and grill for about 5 minutes per side, brushing again with barbecue sauce, until slightly blackened. Cut into serving-size pieces.

Nutrition Per Serving: *717 calories, 45g total fat, 16g sat fat, 276mg cholesterol, 261mg sodium, 2g carbohydrate, 1g fiber, 73g protein*

Jennifer Weber, Williamsville, NY

Grilled Veggie Combo

My husband and I created this recipe together when we planted our first garden.

Makes 4 servings

1 zucchini, thinly sliced
1 yellow squash, thinly sliced
1 red onion, thinly sliced
1 T. garlic, minced
1 T. olive oil
fresh basil, oregano or parsley to taste, chopped

Coat inside of a vegetable grill basket with non-stick vegetable spray; fill with vegetables and garlic. Place on a grill preheated to medium heat. Cover and cook until vegetables are crisp-tender. Remove from grill; transfer vegetables to a serving dish. Lightly drizzle with oil; add desired chopped herbs and serve immediately.

Nutrition Per Serving: *52 calories, 4g total fat, 1g sat fat, 0mg cholesterol, 3mg sodium, 5g carbohydrate, 1g fiber, 1g protein*

Grilled Veggie Combo

Katie Majeske, Denver, PA

Sizzling Bacon Asparagus

Fresh asparagus in the spring is the best...such a delicacy!

Makes 4 servings

16 spears asparagus, trimmed
2 to 3 t. olive oil
pepper to taste
4 slices bacon

Arrange asparagus on a baking sheet. Lightly drizzle with olive oil; sprinkle with pepper. Make a bundle with 4 spears; wrap in a slice of bacon. Secure with wooden toothpicks, if needed. Repeat with remaining ingredients to make 4 bundles. Place on an oiled grate over medium-high heat. Cook for 10 to 12 minutes, turning occasionally, until asparagus is tender and bacon is crisp.

Nutrition Per Serving: *79 calories, 6g total fat, 1g sat fat, 9mg cholesterol, 189mg sodium, 3g carbohydrate, 1g fiber, 4g protein*

Ed Smulski, Lyons, IL

Pork & Peach Kabobs

These kabobs are so tasty and so pretty. We serve them for special outdoor gatherings and they are always a hit!

Makes 6 servings

2 peaches, halved, pitted and cut
    into 6 wedges
1 sweet onion, cut into 6 wedges
1-1/2 lbs. pork tenderloin, cut into
    18 to 20 cubes
6 skewers, soaked in water
3/4 c. honey barbecue sauce

Cut peach and onion wedges crosswise in half. Thread peach, onion and pork pieces alternately onto skewers, leaving some space in between for even grilling. Grill skewers over medium-high heat for 15 minutes, or until pork juices run clear, turning skewers occasionally. Brush with barbecue sauce during the last 5 minutes.

Nutrition Per Serving: *194 calories, 3g total fat, 1g sat fat, 73mg cholesterol, 297mg sodium, 18g carbohydrate, 2g fiber, 24g protein*

Pork & Peach Kabobs

Sherry Gordon, Arlington Heights, IL

Yummy Meatball Skewers

My kids love these skewers! What's more fun than dinner on a stick? Sometimes we add cherry tomatoes and zucchini chunks too.

Serves 10

28-oz. pkg. frozen meatballs, thawed
2 green and/or red peppers, cut into 1-inch squares
2 c. pineapple cubes
1 red onion, cut into 1-inch squares
10 skewers, soaked in water
1-1/2 c. teriyaki sauce

Place 3 meatballs on each skewer, alternating with pepper, pineapple and onion pieces. Place skewers on a grill over medium heat. Cook for 10 to 12 minutes, turning skewers occasionally. Brush with sauce during last 5 minutes of grilling.

Nutrition Per Serving: *304 calories, 21g total fat, 9g sat fat, 40mg cholesterol, 1625mg sodium, 17g carbohydrate, 2g fiber, 17g protein*

Diana Chaney, Olathe, KS

Savory Flat-Iron Steak

This cut of beef is flavorful and budget-friendly...I'm glad I gave it a try!

Serves 6

1-1/2 lbs. beef flat-iron steak or top blade steak
1/4 c. olive oil
2 T. balsamic vinegar
2 cloves garlic, pressed
1 t. Italian seasoning
salt and pepper to taste

Place steak in a large plastic zipping bag; set aside. Whisk together remaining ingredients in a small bowl; pour over steak. Close bag; refrigerate for one to 8 hours, turning occasionally. Drain, discarding marinade. Place steak on an oiled grate over medium-high heat; grill for 5 minutes. Turn steak over; move to a slightly cooler part of grill. Grill about 4 minutes, to medium-rare or medium. Remove steak to a serving platter; let stand for several minutes. To serve, thinly slice steak across the grain.

Nutrition Per Serving: *197 calories, 12g total fat, 4g sat fat, 74mg cholesterol, 83mg sodium, 0g carbohydrate, 0g fiber, 21g protein*

Savory Flat-Iron Steak

Kristin Pittis Dennison, OH

Sweet & Spicy Chicken

This chicken is delicious! Serve with a baked potato and steamed fresh green beans for a dinner you'll love.

Makes 4 servings

1/2 c. light brown sugar, packed
2 T. chili powder
1 t. seasoned salt
1/2 t. garlic powder
4 boneless, skinless chicken breasts

In a large plastic zipping bag, combine all ingredients except chicken. Pat chicken dry; add to bag. Seal bag and rub brown sugar mixture into chicken. Refrigerate for at least 30 minutes. Place chicken on an oiled grate over medium-high heat. Grill for 8 to 10 minutes on each side, until chicken juices run clear.

Nutrition Per Serving: *204 calories, 2g total fat, 1g sat fat, 65mg cholesterol, 583mg sodium, 20g carbohydrate, 1g fiber, 26g protein*

Irene Robinson, Cincinnati, OH

Irene's Portabella Burgers

Scrumptious...I promise you won't miss the meat! Serve on pretzel buns to bring out the beauty of the mushrooms. If you don't wish to fire up the grill, use a heavy grill skillet on your stovetop. However you make this amazing sandwich, your family will love it and won't believe the wonderful flavor and texture of this meatless sandwich.

Serves 4

4 portabella mushroom caps
1 c. Italian salad dressing
4 pretzel or sourdough buns, split
4 slices Muenster or Gruyère cheese
Garnish: romaine lettuce or arugula

Combine mushrooms and salad dressing in a plastic zipping bag, turning to coat. Chill 30 minutes, turning occasionally. Remove mushrooms, discarding dressing. Grill mushrooms, covered with grill lid, over medium heat for 2 to 3 minutes on each side. Grill buns, cut-side down, one minute, or until toasted. Top buns with mushroom, cheese and lettuce or arugula; serve immediately.

Nutrition Per Serving: *334 calories, 15g total fat, 6g sat fat, 27mg cholesterol, 731mg sodium, 36g carbohydrate, 3g fiber, 14g protein*

Irene's Portabella Burgers

Erin Brock, Charleston, WV

Lemony Grilled Broccoli

Delicious! My picky kid who won't eat steamed broccoli gobbles it up when it's fixed this way.

Serves 4 to 6

2-1/2 T. lemon juice
2 T. olive oil
1/4 t. salt
1/4 t. pepper
1 bunch broccoli, cut into spears
   and trimmed
3/4 c. grated Parmesan cheese

In a large bowl, whisk together lemon juice, oil, salt and pepper; add broccoli and toss to coat. Let stand for 30 minutes. Toss broccoli again; drain and discard marinade. Place cheese in a large plastic zipping bag. Add broccoli, a few pieces at a time; shake to coat. Grill broccoli, covered, on an oiled grate over medium heat for 8 to 10 minutes on each side, until crisp-tender.

Nutrition Per Serving: *115 calories, 7g total fat, 3g sat fat, 10mg cholesterol, 289mg sodium, 7g carbohydrate, 3g fiber, 7g protein*

Miriam Schultz, Ft. Meyers, FL

Spiced-Up Grilled Zucchini

I always have an abundance of zucchini in my garden in the summertime. We love it cooked so many ways, but this grilled recipe has just the right zing!

Serves 4

3 medium-size zucchini sliced into
   1/2-inch planks
1 T. olive oil
1 T. red pepper flakes
1/2 t. salt
1/2 t. pepper
2 T. Feta cheese
2 T. balsamic vinegar dressing

Lay zucchini on paper towel to remove in excess moisture. Pat dry. Brush with olive oil and sprinkle with red pepper flakes, salt and pepper. Place on oiled grill grates and grill until tender, about 5 minutes. Remove from heat and put on platter. Sprinkle with Feta cheese and dressing. Serve immediately.

Nutrition Per Serving: *87 calories, 7g total fat, 2g sat fat, 4mg cholesterol, 478mg sodium, 6g carbohydrate, 2g fiber, 3g protein*

Spiced-Up Grilled Zucchini

Teresa Willett, Ontario, Canada

Grilled Zucchini Wraps

We like to make wraps for a quick lunch. Sometimes I have the chicken grilled the night before, so all I have to do is make the wrap. So simple!

Makes 8 servings

4 boneless, skinless chicken breasts
4 to 6 zucchini, sliced lengthwise
  into 1/4-inch thick slices
olive oil to taste
salt and pepper to taste
1/2 c. ranch salad dressing, divided
8 10-inch whole-grain flour tortillas
8 leaves lettuce
Garnish: shredded Cheddar cheese

Brush chicken and zucchini with olive oil; sprinkle with salt and pepper. Grill chicken over medium-high heat for 5 minutes. Turn chicken over; add zucchini to grill. Grill 5 minutes longer, or until chicken juices run clear and zucchini is tender. Slice chicken into strips; set aside. For each wrap, spread one tablespoon salad dressing on a tortilla. Top with a lettuce leaf, 1/2 cup chicken and 3 to 4 slices of zucchini. Sprinkle with cheese; roll up.

Nutrition Per Serving: *307 calories, 12g total fat, 2g sat fat, 37mg cholesterol, 444mg sodium, 31g carbohydrate, 4g fiber, 20g protein*

Diane Axtell, Marble Falls, TX

Grilled Romaine Salad

When my neighbor told me I could grill romaine lettuce, I could hardly believe it...but I tried it and we all love it! It reminds me of a wilted lettuce salad my mother used to make.

Serves 2

10 large leaves romaine lettuce,
  trimmed
1 T. olive oil
1/2 t. salt
1/2 t. pepper
1 c. cherry tomatoes
3 slices bacon, crisply cooked
1/2 c. shredded Parmesan cheese

Brush leaves with oil and sprinkle with salt and pepper. Place the lettuce leaves on oiled grill grates over medium-high heat turned as soon as any char is visible. Grill for about 4 minutes. Remove from heat and layer on a serving dish with tomatoes, bacon and cheese. Serve immediately.

Nutrition Per Serving: *242 calories, 18g total fat, 6g sat fat, 28mg cholesterol, 1218mg sodium, 8g carbohydrate, 4g fiber, 14g protein*

Grilled Romaine Salad

Kelly Greene, Riverside, CA

Rich's Charcoal Lemon-Lime Chicken

This recipe is my stepdad's. It is always requested when we go to visit him...terrific for tailgating!

Serves 6

6 boneless, skinless chicken breasts
1/2 c. brown sugar, packed
1/4 c. cider vinegar
3 T. coarse mustard
juice of 1 lime
Optional: 1 clove garlic, pressed
1 t. salt, or to taste
pepper to taste
6 T. oil
Garnish: lemon slices, chopped
    fresh herbs

Place chicken in a large plastic zipping bag; set aside. In a bowl, combine remaining ingredients except oil and garnish. Blend well; whisk in oil. Add marinade to chicken; seal bag. Refrigerate for 8 hours to overnight, turning occasionally. One hour before serving time, bring chicken to room temperature, discarding marinade. Place chicken on an oiled grate over medium-high heat. Grill 4 minutes per side. Garnish as desired.

Nutrition Per Serving: *180 calories, 6g total fat, 1g sat fat, 65mg cholesterol, 113mg sodium, 4g carbohydrate, 0g fiber, 26g protein*

Nancy Molldrem, Eau Claire, WI

Grilled Parmesan Bread

Crisp toasted cheesy bread...yum! We make it every time we grill.

Serves 6

1/4 c. butter, softened
1 T. fresh herbs such as basil or
    rosemary
1/2 c. grated Parmesan cheese
6 slices whole-grain French bread,
    cut one-inch thick on the diagonal

Blend butter, herbs and cheese in a small bowl. Spread mixture on both sides of bread slices. Place on grill over medium heat. Toast until golden, about 3 minutes on each side.

Nutrition Per Serving: *212 calories, 12g total fat, 7g sat fat, 27mg cholesterol, 302mg sodium, 18g carbohydrate, 3g fiber, 9g protein*

KITCHEN TIP:
If you like the taste of freshly grated Parmesan cheese, grate it from a block of cheese and keep it in the freezer. It tastes fresher than cheese in a purchased container.

Grilled Parmesan Bread

Lynn Daniel, Portage, MI

Yummy Blue Cheese Burgers

These mouthwatering burgers will be a hit at your next cookout.

Serves 6

2 lbs. ground beef
Cajun seasoning to taste
1/2 c. half-and-half
Optional: 1 t. dried basil
4-oz. container crumbled blue
cheese
6 kaiser rolls, split and toasted
Optional: sliced red onion, butter

Form ground beef into 6 patties; sprinkle with Cajun seasoning to taste. Grill to desired doneness. Combine half-and-half and basil, if using, in a saucepan. Bring to a boil; simmer until thickened and reduced by half. Add blue cheese; stir just until melted. Place burgers on rolls; spoon sauce over burgers. If desired, sauté red onion in butter until tender; spoon onto burgers.

Nutrition Per Serving: *522 calories, 25g total fat, 11g sat fat, 119mg cholesterol, 677mg sodium, 31g carbohydrate, 1g fiber, 40g protein*

Noah Burnley, Ankeny, IA

Simply-Grilled Peaches

Summer means fresh fruit...and nothing is better than a fresh peach grilled just long enough to bring out that sweet flavor!

Serves 8

4 large Colorado or other freestone
peaches, halved and pitted
juice of one lemon
1 T. olive oil
Optional: sugar and cinnamon

Cut the peaches in half and carefully remove the seed. Brush cut sides of peaches with lemon juice and olive oil. Place peaches cut-side down on a oiled, medium-hot grill. Grill for about 6 minutes without turning. Remove from heat; sprinkle with sugar and cinnamon if desired.

Nutrition Per Serving: *44 calories, 2g total fat, 0g sat fat, 0mg cholesterol, 0mg sodium, 9g carbohydrate, 1g fiber, 1g protein*

Simply-Grilled Peaches

Tomato Tart, p. 136

CHAPTER FOUR

SIMPLE
Salads & Sides

Orange-Wild Rice Chicken Salad, p. 132   Chili Sweet Potato Fries, p. 130

Jo Ann, Gooseberry Patch

Fried Pecan Okra

You can use a 16-ounce package of frozen cut okra, thawed, if you'd rather have bite-size pieces.

Serves 8

1 c. pecans, chopped
1-1/2 c. low-salt biscuit baking mix
1/2 t. salt
1/2 t. pepper
2 10-oz. pkgs. frozen whole okra, thawed
peanut oil for frying

Place pecans in an even layer in a shallow pan. Bake at 350 degrees for 10 minutes or until lightly toasted, stirring occasionally. Process pecans, baking mix, salt and pepper in a food processor until nuts are finely ground. Place pecan mixture in a large bowl. Add okra, tossing to coat. Gently press pecan mixture into okra. Pour oil to a depth of about 2 inches into a Dutch oven or cast-iron skillet; heat to 350 degrees. Fry okra, in batches, turning once, for 5 to 6 minutes, until golden; drain on paper towels.

Nutrition Per Serving: *335 calories, 28g total fat, 4g sat fat, 0mg cholesterol, 362mg sodium, 21g carbohydrate, 3g fiber, 4g protein*

Carol Field Dahlstrom, Ankeny, IA

Asparagus Pasta Salad

This salad welcomes spring with beautiful colors, textures and flavors.

Makes 4 servings

8 c. fresh greens such as arugula, baby spinach, baby romaine lettuce
1 c. cherry tomatoes, halved
1 c. whole-grain spaghetti, cooked
1 lb. fresh asparagus, blanched
Optional: crumbled feta cheese
favorite vinaigrette dressing to taste

Place greens and tomatoes in a large salad bowl. Toss lightly. Divide among 4 salad plates. Add spaghetti and asparagus to each plate. Garnish with feta cheese, if desired. Drizzle with dressing. Serve immediately.

Nutrition Per Serving: *84 calories, 1g total fat, 0g sat fat, 0mg cholesterol, 34mg sodium, 17g carbohydrate, 5g fiber, 6g protein*

Asparagus Pasta Salad

Tamara Parlor, Hazelhurst, GA

Cabbage-Tomato Slaw

This slaw is so easy to make and yet it is one of our family favorites. I oftentimes purchase the cabbage already shredded to save time.

Makes 8 servings

1 head cabbage, chopped
1 sweet onion, chopped
2 tomatoes, diced
1/2 c. mayonnaise
salt and pepper to taste

Combine all ingredients in a large salad bowl. Toss to mix; cover and refrigerate until serving time. Toss again before serving.

Nutrition Per Serving: *156 calories, 11g total fat, 2g sat fat, 5mg cholesterol, 111mg sodium, 14g carbohydrate, 5g fiber, 3g protein*

Beth Flack, Terre Haute, IN

Caprese Salad

Very refreshing! This is one of my favorite summer salads and it is pretty and easy to make.

Serves 6

2 beefsteak tomatoes, sliced
4-oz. pkg. fresh mozzarella cheese, sliced
8 leaves fresh basil
Italian salad dressing to taste

Layer tomatoes, cheese slices and basil leaves in rows or in a circle around a large platter. Sprinkle with salad dressing. Cover and chill for one hour before serving.

Nutrition Per Serving: *72 calories, 4g total fat, 3g sat fat, 15mg cholesterol, 123mg sodium, 4g carbohydrate, 1g fiber, 2g sugars, 5g protein*

GOOD TO KNOW
Tomatoes contain lycopene, a powerful antioxidant. Ripe, red tomatoes tend to carry more of this antioxidant than green or under-ripe tomatoes.

Caprese Salad

Jo Ann, Gooseberry Patch

Easy Fancy Broccoli

What an easy dish to make and it tastes delightful!

Makes 6 servings

2 T. pine nuts
1 T. butter
1 T. olive oil
6 cloves garlic, thinly sliced
1 lb. broccoli flowerets
1/8 t. salt
1/8 t. red pepper flakes

Toast pine nuts in a large skillet over medium heat 6 minutes or until golden. Remove from skillet and set aside. Heat butter and oil in same skillet over medium heat until butter melts. Add garlic; sauté one to 2 minutes or until golden. Add broccoli, salt and red pepper flakes. Sauté 8 minutes, until broccoli is tender. Stir in pine nuts before serving.

Nutrition Per Serving: *86 calories, 6g total fat, 2g sat fat, 5mg cholesterol, 75mg sodium, 6g carbohydrate, 2g fiber, 3g protein*

Jackie Crough, Salina, KS

Carrot-Raisin Salad

Grandma made this salad often. It's always very good!

Makes 6 servings

3 c. carrots, peeled and shredded
3/4 c. raisins
1/4 c. chopped walnuts
1/3 c. light mayonnaise

Mix together all ingredients in a large bowl. Serve immediately or cover and refrigerate overnight.

Nutrition Per Serving: *148 calories, 6g total fat, 1g sat fat, 2mg cholesterol, 149mg sodium, 23g carbohydrate, 3g fiber, 15g sugars, 2g protein*

Carrot-Raisin Salad

Brandi Joiner, Minot, ND

Pasta Puttanesca

Such a versatile recipe! It's good either warm or cold.

Serves 6

16-oz. pkg. rotini pasta, uncooked
1 red onion, chopped
1 T. olive oil
5-oz. jar sliced green olives with
    pimentos, drained
4-oz. can sliced black olives, drained
24-oz. jar low-sodium marinara
    sauce
Garnish: grated Parmesan cheese

Cook pasta according to package directions; drain. Meanwhile, in a large skillet over medium heat, sauté onion in olive oil until soft. Add olives; continue to sauté for another 2 to 3 minutes. Add pasta to the skillet and toss to mix. Add marinara sauce; stir well and heat through. Garnish with Parmesan cheese.

Nutrition Per Serving: *463 calories, 13g total fat, 2g sat fat, 0mg cholesterol, 692mg sodium, 75g carbohydrate, 7g fiber, 12g protein*

Marsha Pounds, Rolla, MO

Favorite Stir-Fried Zucchini

Toasted pine nuts on the top make this extra yummy!

Makes 4 servings

1 T. olive oil
1 lb. zucchini, cut lengthwise into
    strips
1 onion, thinly sliced
1 T. sesame seed
1 T. reduced-sodium soy sauce
1/8 t. sea salt
Garnish: toasted pine nuts

Heat oil in a skillet over medium heat; add zucchini and onion. Cook for 5 to 10 minutes, stirring frequently, until crisp-tender. Quickly stir in sesame seed, soy sauce and salt. Heat through and serve promptly. Garnish as desired.

Nutrition Per Serving: *63 calories, 4g total fat, 1g sat fat, 0mg cholesterol, 192mg sodium, 7g carbohydrate, 2g fiber, 2g protein*

Favorite Stir-Fried Zucchini

Jolene Koval, Ontario, Canada

Jolene's Chickpea Medley

This unusual salad goes together in a jiffy! It's terrific for warm-weather meals grilled in the backyard.

Makes 6 servings

15-oz. can low-sodium garbanzo
    beans, drained and rinsed
1 red pepper, diced
1 c. kale, finely shredded
1 zucchini, chopped
1 ear corn, kernels cut off, or
    1/2 c. frozen corn, thawed
1/4 c. reduced-fat Italian salad
    dressing

In a salad bowl, combine beans and vegetables. Drizzle with salad dressing; toss to mix. Let stand 15 minutes before serving to allow flavors to blend.

Nutrition Per Serving: *149 calories, 3g total fat, 0g sat fat, 0mg cholesterol, 14mg sodium, 25g carbohydrate, 6g fiber, 7g protein*

Cyndy DeStefano, Mercer, PA

Feta Green Beans

This is such a great side dish. Frozen green beans are so handy, but this dish is especially good with green beans right from the garden!

Makes 10 servings

16-oz. pkg. frozen green beans
2 T. butter
16-oz. pkg. sliced mushrooms
1 onion, finely diced
2 cloves garlic, minced
1/4 t. salt
1/2 t. pepper
4-oz. container crumbled reduced-
    fat feta cheese

Prepare green beans according to package directions; drain. Melt butter in a large skillet over medium heat. Add mushrooms, onion, garlic, salt and pepper. Cook 5 to 7 minutes, until heated through. Stir in cheese. Serve immediately.

Nutrition Per Serving: *62 calories, 4g total fat, 3g sat fat, 10mg cholesterol, 200mg sodium, 5g carbohydrate, 2g fiber, 4g protein*

Feta Green Beans

Angela Murphy, Tempe, AZ.

Dijon-Ginger Carrots

The hint of ginger in these carrots makes them hard to resist. Even the kids will love them!

Makes 12 servings

12 carrots, peeled and sliced
   1/4-inch thick
1/3 c. Dijon mustard
1/2 c. brown sugar, packed
1 t. fresh ginger, peeled and minced
1/4 t. salt
1/8 t. pepper

Combine all ingredients in a slow cooker; stir. Cover and cook on high setting for 2 to 3 hours, until carrots are tender, stirring twice during cooking.

Nutrition Per Serving: *71 calories, 0g total fat, 0g sat fat, 0mg cholesterol, 261mg sodium, 16g carbohydrate, 2g fiber, 1g protein*

Carol Field Dahlstrom, Ankeny, IA

Fresh-as-Spring Salad

Who can resist a bed of fresh greens topped with sliced strawberries and a splash of balsamic dressing? Make your own dressing or choose your favorite store-bought variety.

Makes 4 servings

8 c. fresh greens such as arugula, baby spinach, baby romaine lettuce
1 c. strawberries, hulled and sliced
1 c. sweetened, dried cranberries
1/2 c. celery, chopped
1/2 c. toasted pine nuts
Optional: shaved Parmesan cheese

Place greens in a large salad bowl. Add strawberries, cranberries and celery; toss lightly. Sprinkle with pine nuts. Drizzle with Balsamic Vinaigrette Dressing and toss again. Divide among 4 salad plates. Garnish with Parmesan cheese, if desired. Serve immediately.

Nutrition Per Serving: *233 calories, 12g total fat, 1g sat fat, 0mg cholesterol, 41mg sodium, 32g carbohydrate, 4g fiber, 4g protein*

BALSAMIC VINAIGRETTE DRESSING:
1/4 c. balsamic vinegar
1/2 c. extra-virgin olive oil
1 T. honey
1 T. lime juice
1 T. fresh parsley, minced

Combine all ingredients in a small jar with a tight-sealing lid. Add lid and shake until blended. Refrigerate, if making ahead of time; chilled dressing will have a thicker consistency.

Nutrition Per Serving: *259 calories, 27g total fat, 4g sat fat, 0mg cholesterol, 2mg sodium, 5g carbohydrate, 0g fiber, 0g protein*

Fresh-as-Spring Salad

Cathy Hillier, Salt Lake City, UT

Peppers & Pierogies

This tasty version of pierogies and peppers makes a great side dish for grilled meat of any kind.

Serves 4

10-oz. pkg. frozen potato and onion
    pierogies
16-oz. pkg. frozen stir-fry peppers
    and onions
8-oz. can tomato sauce
salt and pepper to taste

Cook pierogies according to package directions. Drain, reserving 1/2 cup of cooking liquid; cover pierogies to keep warm. Spray a large skillet with non-stick vegetable spray. Add frozen vegetables; cook until tender and golden and most of the liquid is cooked off. Stir in tomato sauce and reserved liquid; heat through. Toss vegetable mixture with pierogies; season with salt and pepper.

Nutrition Per Serving: *231 calories, 2g total fat, 0g sat fat, 0mg cholesterol, 513mg sodium, 48g carbohydrate, 5g fiber, 9g protein*

Michelle Powell, Valley, AL

Comforting Creamed Corn

This recipe calls for frozen corn, but if you have fresh corn, just cook it and cut it off the cob and use that instead of frozen. Either way, this is a wonderful side dish!

Makes 8 servings

1 T. butter
4 c. corn, thawed if frozen
1/2 c. plain Greek yogurt
2 T. grated Parmesan cheese
1 t. dried basil

Melt butter in a non-stick skillet over medium heat; add corn. Cook for about 6 minutes, stirring occasionally, until tender. Reduce heat; stir in yogurt and cook for 4 minutes. Stir in cheese and basil just before serving.

Nutrition Per Serving: *88 calories, 2g total fat, 1g sat fat, 6mg cholesterol, 39mg sodium, 15g carbohydrate, 1g fiber, 4g protein*

Comforting Creamed Corn

Alma Evans, Patrick AFB, FL

Chunky Tomato-Avocado Salad

Let it sit for at least 2 hours if you don't have time to refrigerate overnight. The flavors blend so nicely that way.

Makes 4 servings

1 avocado, pitted, peeled and cubed
3 plum tomatoes, chopped
1/4 c. sweet onion, chopped
1 T. fresh cilantro, chopped
2 to 3 T. lemon juice

Gently stir ingredients together; cover and refrigerate overnight.

Nutrition Per Serving: *80 calories, 5g total fat, 1g sat fat, 0mg cholesterol, 8mg sodium, 9g carbohydrate, 3g fiber, 1g protein*

Stephanie Pulkownik,
South Milwaukee, WI

Citrus & Beet Spinach Salad

This colorful salad is festive enough for fancy celebrations or for everyday meals. Make your own dressing or serve with one you love.

Makes 8 servings

10-oz. pkg. baby spinach
2-1/2 c. beets, cooked, peeled and diced
2 oranges, sectioned and seeds removed
1/2 c. red onion, thinly sliced
1/3 c. chopped walnuts, toasted

In a large salad bowl, combine all ingredients except salad dressing. Add 1/2 cup Raspberry Vinaigrette Dressing immediately before serving; toss again and serve.

Nutrition Per Serving: *76 calories, 3g total fat, 0g sat fat, 0mg cholesterol, 62mg sodium, 10g carbohydrate, 3g fiber, 3g protein*

RASPBERRY VINAIGRETTE DRESSING:
Makes 16 servings

1/3 c. canola oil
2 T. water
2/3 c. raspberry vinegar
1 t. sugar
1/4 t. salt
1 t. pepper

Whisk all ingredients together. Store any unused dressing in refrigerator. Makes one cup.

Nutrition Per Serving: *43 calories, 4g total fat, 0g sat fat, 0mg cholesterol, 38mg sodium, 0g carbohydrate, 0g fiber, 0g protein*

Citrus & Beet Spinach Salad

Judy Spahn, Canton, IL

15-Minute Parmesan Pasta

I like to serve this very quick pasta dish with grilled pork chops or chicken. The entire bowl of pasta is always gone by the end of the meal! Add a platter of toasted garlic bread to make the meal complete.

Makes 4 servings

8-oz. pkg. pasta, cooked
1 clove garlic, minced
1/4 c. olive oil
3/4 c. grated Parmesan cheese

Place pasta in a large serving bowl; keep warm. Sauté garlic in olive oil until golden and tender; pour over pasta. Add cheese; toss gently to coat. Serve immediately.

Nutrition Per Serving: *408 calories, 20g total fat, 5g sat fat, 17mg cholesterol, 290mg sodium, 43g carbohydrate, 2g fiber, 15g protein*

Liz Plotnick-Snay, Gooseberry Patch

Mandarin Orange Salad with Raspberry Vinaigrette

Quick & easy to prepare, this salad is best topped with a sweet dressing like Raspberry Vinaigrette.

Makes 4 servings

4 c. green or red leaf lettuce, torn
    into bite-size pieces
3 mandarin oranges, peeled and
    sectioned
1/2 c. walnut pieces, toasted
1/2 red onion, sliced

Combine all ingredients. Toss with 1/4 cup Raspberry Vinaigrette dressing.

Nutrition Per Serving: *134 calories, 8g total fat, 1g sat fat, 0mg cholesterol, 43mg sodium, 16g carbohydrate, 3g fiber, 2g protein.*

RASPBERRY VINAIGRETTE:
Makes 16 servings

1/2 c. raspberry vinegar
1/4 c. seedless raspberry jam
1 t. coriander or ground cumin
1/4 t. salt
1/4 t. pepper
1/2 c. extra-virgin olive oil

Combine first 5 ingredients in blender. Turn blender on high; gradually add oil. Chill. Makes 1-1/4 cups.

Nutrition Per Serving: *81 calories, 7g total fat, 1g sat fat, 0mg cholesterol, 41mg sodium, 5g carbohydrate, 0g fiber, 0g protein*

Mandarin Orange Salad with Raspberry Vinaigrette

Tracey Zimmerman, Spirit Lake, IA

Chili Sweet Potato Fries

This is a great way to get the kids to eat sweet potatoes. They will love them!

Serves 10

3-1/2 lbs. sweet potatoes, sliced into
   1-inch wedges
2 T. olive oil
3/4 t. salt
1/4 t. pepper
1/2 c. orange juice
1 T. honey
2 t. chili powder

Place potato wedges in a large plastic zipping bag; sprinkle with oil, salt and pepper. Toss to mix. Arrange potato wedges on lightly greased baking sheets. Stir together orange juice, honey and chili powder; set aside. Bake, uncovered, at 450 degrees for 25 to 30 minutes, until tender, shaking pans and basting with orange juice mixture several times.

Nutrition Per Serving: *166 calories, 3g total fat, 0g sat fat, 0mg cholesterol, 258mg sodium, 33g carbohydrate, 5g fiber, 3g protein*

Joan White, Malvern, PA

Simple Scalloped Tomatoes

This tangy-sweet dish makes a delicious dinner. Serve with cheese bread for a complete meal.

Serves 6

1 onion, chopped
1/4 c. butter
28-oz. can low-sodium diced
   tomatoes
5 slices bread, lightly toasted and
   cubed
1/4 c. brown sugar, packed
1/2 t. salt
1/4 t. pepper

In a skillet over medium heat, cook onion in butter until just tender, but not browned. Combine onion mixture with tomatoes and their juice in a bowl; add remaining ingredients, and mix well. Pour into a greased 8"x8" baking pan. Bake, uncovered, at 350 degrees for 45 minutes.

Nutrition Per Serving: *196 calories, 9g total fat, 5g sat fat, 21mg cholesterol, 323mg sodium, 28g carbohydrate, 2g fiber, 3g protein*

Simple Scalloped Tomatoes

Wendy Reaume, Ontario, Canada

Cheesy Chile Rice

When I was growing up, my mom made this simple rice dish whenever we had Mexican food for dinner.

Makes 6 servings

2 c. water
2 c. instant rice, uncooked
16-oz. container low-fat sour cream
4-oz. can diced green chiles
2 c. shredded Cheddar cheese, divided

In a saucepan over medium-high heat, bring water to a boil. Stir in rice; remove from heat. Cover and let stand 5 minutes, until water is absorbed. In a large bowl, mix together rice, sour cream, chiles and 2 cups cheese. Spread in a greased 2-quart casserole dish; top with remaining cheese. Bake, uncovered, at 400 degrees for 30 minutes, or until cheese is melted and top is lightly golden.

Nutrition Per Serving: *412 calories, 23g total fat, 15g sat fat, 66mg cholesterol, 352mg sodium,33g carbohydrate, 1g fiber, 17g protein*

Rhonda Reeder, Ellicott City, MD

Orange-Wild Rice Chicken Salad

Heads up! This isn't your ordinary chicken salad...it's better! This salad boasts wild rice, sugar snap peas and mandarin oranges.

Makes 5 servings

1 c. wild rice, cooked
2 c. cooked chicken breast, cubed
1 c. sugar snap peas, trimmed
15-oz. can mandarin oranges, drained
Optional: lettuce leaves

Combine all ingredients except lettuce in a large bowl, adding 1/3 cup Honey-Dijon Salad dressing; mix well. Cover and chill until serving time. Serve on lettuce if desired.

Nutrition per serving: *269 calories, 10g fat, 1g sat fat, 48mg cholesterol, 85mg sodium, 25g carbohydrate, 2g fiber, 19g protein*

HONEY-DIJON SALAD DRESSING:
Makes 16 servings

1/2 c. canola oil
3 T. honey
3 T. lemon juice
1 T. light mayonnaise
2 T. Dijon mustard

Whisk all ingredients together. Remix before serving. Chill any remaining dressing. Makes one cup.

Nutrition Per Serving: *77 calories, 7g total fat, 1g sat fat, 0mg cholesterol, 33mg sodium, 4g carbohydrate, 0g fiber, 0g protein*

Orange-Wild Rice Chicken Salad

Paula Smith, Ottawa, IL

Quick & Easy Parmesan Asparagus

This recipe really is quick to make and it is always a hit. Add a sprinkle of toasted sesame seed for a little extra crunch.

Serves 10

4 lbs. asparagus, trimmed
1/4 c. butter, melted
2 c. shredded Parmesan cheese
1 t. salt
1/2 t. pepper

To a large skillet, add asparagus and one inch of water. Bring to a boil. Reduce heat; cover and simmer for 5 to 7 minutes, until crisp-tender. Drain and arrange asparagus in a greased 13"x9" baking pan. Drizzle with butter; sprinkle with Parmesan cheese, salt and pepper. Bake, uncovered, at 350 degrees for 10 to 15 minutes, until cheese is melted.

Nutrition Per Serving: *134 calories, 9g total fat, 6g sat fat, 24mg cholesterol, 507mg sodium, 6g carbohydrate, 3g fiber, 9g protein*

Beverly Brown, Bowie, MD

Marinated Broccoli Salad

So easy...you can mix in the bag! Be sure to let the flavors blend overnight.

Makes 8 servings

3 bunches broccoli flowerets, chopped
1 t. dill weed
2 T. canola oil
1/4 c. red wine vinegar
2 cloves garlic, minced
2 T. unsweetened dried cranberries

Place ingredients in a one-gallon plastic zipping bag; close and shake well. Refrigerate overnight, shaking occasionally; serve chilled.

Nutrition Per Serving: *61 calories, 4g total fat, 0g sat fat, 0mg cholesterol, 22mg sodium, 6g carbohydrate, 0g fiber, 2g protein*

Marinated Broccoli Salad

Virginia Shaw, Medon, TN

Mama's Cucumber Salad

I used to take this salad to my sons' baseball award dinners and picnics. Children and adults alike always request this salad...it's cool, refreshing and very simple to make.

Makes 10 servings

2 cucumbers, sliced
1 bunch green onions, diced, or
   1 red onion, sliced and separated
   into rings
Optional: 2 to 3 tomatoes, diced
1/2 c. zesty Italian salad dressing

Toss together vegetables in a large bowl; pour salad dressing over all and toss to mix. Cover and refrigerate at least 3 hours to overnight.

Nutrition Per Serving: *61 calories, 4g total fat, 1g sat fat, 0mg cholesterol, 200mg sodium, 7g carbohydrate, 1g fiber, 1g protein*

Andy Neymeyer, Des Moines, IA

Tomato Tart

Purchased frozen flatbread makes this recipe so quick to make and so yummy. Choose both red and yellow tomatoes for a beautiful presentation.

Serves 6

6-oz. pkg. frozen flatbread, thawed
2 T. Dijon mustard
3 oz. Brie cheese, sliced 1/4- inch
   thick
3 c. tomatoes, sliced
1 T. olive oil
1 T. fresh oregano, chopped

Unroll flatbread and press into a 13"x9" sheet pan. Spread mustard on flatbread and top with cheese. Layer fresh tomatoes on top. Drizzle with olive oil and sprinkle with fresh oregano. Bake at 400 degrees for 20 minutes, until bread is golden and cheese is melted. Serve warm or at room temperature.

Nutrition Per Serving: *153 calories, 8g total fat, 3g sat fat, 14mg cholesterol, 256mg sodium, 15g carbohydrate, 2g fiber, 6g protein*

Tomato Tart

Beverly Tanner, Crouse, NC

Old-Fashioned Creamed Corn

Using fresh corn on the cob makes this recipe simply heavenly, but frozen corn can work just as well.

Serves 6

6 ears corn, husked
1/4 c. bacon drippings
1/4 c. water
2 T. all-purpose flour
1/2 c. milk
sugar to taste
salt and pepper to taste

Remove kernels from corn cobs, reserving as much liquid as possible. Set aside. Heat drippings in a cast-iron skillet over medium heat. Add corn and reserved liquid. Stir in water and cook for 15 minutes. Whisk flour into milk; slowly add to corn. Reduce heat to low and cook, stirring frequently, until mixture thickens. Sprinkle with sugar, salt and pepper; stir to blend.

Nutrition Per Serving: *162 calories, 10g total fat, 5g sat fat, 11mg cholesterol, 62mg sodium, 17g carbohydrate, 1g fiber, 3g protein*

Ann Farris, Biscoe, AR

Lemon-Garlic Brussels Sprouts

When you sauté the Brussels sprouts, they turn into little gold nuggets of flavor.

Makes 6 servings

3 T. olive oil
2 lbs. Brussels sprouts, trimmed and halved
3 cloves garlic, minced
zest and juice of 1 lemon
sea salt and pepper to taste
3 T. Gruyère cheese, grated

Heat oil in a large skillet over medium-high heat. Add Brussels sprouts; sauté for 7 to 8 minutes. Turn sprouts over; sprinkle with garlic. Continue cooking 7 to 8 minutes, until sprouts are golden, caramelized and tender. Reduce heat to low. Add remaining ingredients except cheese; stir to combine. Adjust seasonings, as needed. Top with cheese just before serving.

Nutrition Per Serving: *95 calories, 4g total fat, 1g sat fat, 3mg cholesterol, 62mg sodium, 9g carbohydrate, 5g fiber, 7g protein*

Lemon-Garlic Brussels Sprouts

Kimberly Pierotti, Milmay, NJ

Creamy Spinach Ravioli

This recipe is so quick to make and is a great addition to any grilled or roasted meat.

Serves 4

25-oz. pkg. frozen cheese ravioli, uncooked
2 9-oz. pkgs. frozen creamed spinach
1/4 c. grated Parmesan cheese to taste
1/4 t. salt
1/4 t. pepper

Prepare ravioli and spinach separately, according to package directions; drain. Place ravioli in a large serving bowl; top with creamed spinach, tossing to coat. Add Parmesan cheese, salt and pepper.

Nutrition Per Serving: *418 calories, 14g total fat, 8g sat fat, 85mg cholesterol, 636mg sodium, 55g carbohydrate, 4g fiber, 20g protein*

Carol Field Dahlstrom, Ankeny, IA

Ranch Chicken Salad

This hearty salad is our family's favorite! You can grill the corn the day before, take it off the cob, and keep in the refrigerator until it is time to build your salad. Yummy!

Makes 4 servings

4 c. fresh greens with herbs such as arugula, baby spinach, baby romaine lettuce, cilantro
1 c. grilled chicken, cubed
1 c. grilled corn, sliced from cob
1 c. Colby Jack cheese cubes
1 c. cherry tomatoes, halved
Optional: favorite ranch dressing

Prepare 4 serving plates. Place greens on plates. Add chicken, corn, cheese and tomatoes. Drizzle with dressing if desired. Serve immediately.

Nutrition Per Serving: *243 calories, 14g total fat, 8g sat fat, 61mg cholesterol, 242mg sodium, 11g carbohydrate, 2g fiber, 20g protein*

Ranch Chicken Salad

SIMPLE SALADS & SIDES

Fern Bruner, Phoenix, AZ

Bacon-Brown Sugar Brussels Sprouts

A delicious way to get your family to enjoy eating this leafy veggie!

Serves 8

4 slices bacon
14-oz. can low-sodium chicken broth
1 T. brown sugar, packed
1 t. salt
1-1/2 lbs. Brussels sprouts, trimmed
 and halved

Cook bacon in a Dutch oven over medium heat for 10 minutes, or until crisp. Remove bacon and drain on paper towels, reserving drippings in pan. Add chicken broth, brown sugar and salt to reserved drippings; bring to a boil. Stir in Brussels sprouts. Cover and cook for 6 to 8 minutes, until tender. Transfer to

a serving bowl using a slotted spoon; sprinkle with crumbled bacon. Serve immediately.

Nutrition Per Serving: *71 calories, 2g total fat, 1g sat fat, 4mg cholesterol, 421mg sodium, 10g carbohydrate, 3g fiber, 5g protein*

Sonja Labbe, Quebec, Canada

Tomato-Basil Couscous Salad

If you want to make this salad gluten-free, use quinoa instead of couscous. Either way it is delicious!

Makes 6 servings

2 c. water
1-1/2 c. couscous, uncooked
1 c. tomatoes, chopped
1/4 c. fresh basil, thinly sliced
1/2 c. olive oil
1/3 c. balsamic vinegar
1/2 t. salt
1/4 t. pepper

In a saucepan over high heat, bring water to a boil. Stir in uncooked couscous; remove from heat. Cover and let stand for 5 minutes, until water is absorbed. Add remaining ingredients and toss to mix. Cover and chill for several hours to overnight.

Nutrition Per Serving: *342 calories, 19g total fat, 3g sat fat, 0mg cholesterol, 203mg sodium, 38g carbohydrate, 3g fiber, 6g protein*

Tomato-Basil Couscous Salad

Simple Tomato Bruschetta, p. 163

CHAPTER FIVE

STARTERS, Snacks & Smoothies

Maple-Glazed Frankies, p. 150

Cucumber-Lime Agua Fresca, p. 154

Erin Brock, Charleston, WV

Pinwheel Starters

Use spinach tortillas to add color to these tasty little appetizers.

Makes 32, serves 16

8-oz. pkg. low-fat cream cheese, softened
2 T. light ranch salad dressing
3 12-inch wheat or spinach tortillas
3/4 c. Kalamata olives, chopped
1 c. carrots, peeled and shredded

Mix together cream cheese and ranch dressing. Spread cream cheese mixture evenly over one side of each tortilla. Stir together olives and carrots. Spoon over cream cheese mixture. Roll up each tortilla jelly-roll style; wrap each in plastic wrap. Chill for at least 2 hours; cut into one-inch slices.

Nutrition Per Serving: *106 calories, 5g total fat, 2g sat fat, 8mg cholesterol, 241mg sodium, 12g carbohydrate, 2g fiber, 3g protein*

Sharon Crider, Lebanon, MO

Barbecue Chicken Wings

Everyone loves these sweet little wings at parties or just for a special appetizer.

Makes 30 servings

3 lbs. trimmed chicken wings
1 c. low-sodium barbecue sauce
1/2 c. water
2 T. honey
2 t. mustard
1-1/2 t. Worcestershire sauce

Arrange chicken pieces on broiler pan. Broil wings 4 to 5 inches from heat, turning once, about 10 minutes until chicken is golden. Place chicken in a 4-quart slow cooker. Combine barbecue sauce, water, honey, mustard and Worcestershire sauce in a bowl; mix well and pour over chicken. Cover and cook on low setting for 2 to 2-1/2 hours.

Nutrition Per Serving: *118 calories, 7g total fat, 2g sat fat, 35mg cholesterol, 51mg sodium, 4g carbohydrate, 0g fiber, 8g protein*

Barbecue Chicken Wings

Julianne Saifullah, Lexington, KY

Mushroom Poppers

I always make these at holiday time and serve them on a long rectangular platter. They disappear fast!

Serves 8

16 mushrooms
2 jalapeño peppers, finely chopped, ribs and seeds removed
1 T. olive oil
2 3-oz. pkgs. cream cheese, softened
1/4 c. shredded Cheddar cheese
4 slices bacon, crisply cooked and crumbled
salt and pepper to taste

Separate mushroom stems from caps; set caps aside. Finely chop stems. In a skillet over medium heat, cook chopped stems and peppers in oil; cook and stir until mushrooms are tender, about 10 minutes. Transfer mushroom mixture to a bowl; stir in cheeses and bacon. Season with salt and pepper. Spoon mushroom mixture generously into reserved mushroom caps; arrange caps in a lightly greased 13"x9" baking pan. Bake, uncovered, at 350 degrees for 15 to 20 minutes, until golden on top.

Nutrition Per Serving: *127 calories, 12g total fat, 6g sat fat, 31mg cholesterol, 184mg sodium, 2g carbohydrate, 0g fiber, 4g protein*

Katie Majeske, Denver, PA

Island Chiller

This is such a refreshing drink to serve at a summer pool party.

Makes 8 servings

10-oz. pkg. frozen strawberries
15-oz. can crushed pineapple
1-1/2 c. orange juice
1-qt. bottle club soda or sparkling water, chilled
Optional: strawberries

In a blender, combine frozen strawberries, pineapple with juice and orange juice. Blend until smooth and frothy. Pour mixture into ice cube trays and freeze. To serve, put 3 cubes into each of 8 tall glasses; add 1/2 cup club soda or sparkling water to each glass. Let stand until mixture becomes slushy. Garnish each glass with a strawberry, if desired.

Nutrition Per Serving: *61 calories, 0g total fat, 0g sat fat, 0mg cholesterol, 36mg sodium, 15g carbohydrate, 1g fiber, 1g protein*

KITCHEN TIP
Sparkling water comes in so many flavors so try using a flavored sparking water in this cool drink.

Island Chiller

Pat Sharrot, Circleville, OH

Fresh-Squeezed Lemonade

There is nothing better than fresh-squeezed lemonade on a hot day. Add a drop of red food coloring if you want some pink lemonade for the kids!

Makes 10 servings

1-3/4 c. sugar
8 c. cold water, divided
6 to 8 lemons
ice cubes
Garnish: lemon slices

Combine sugar and one cup water in a small saucepan. Bring to a boil; stir until sugar dissolves. Cool to room temperature; chill. Juice lemons to measure 1-1/2 cups juice; remove seeds and strain pulp, if desired. In a large pitcher, stir together chilled syrup, juice and remaining water. Chill for several hours to blend flavors. Serve over ice cubes; garnish with lemon slices.

Nutrition Per Serving: *126 calories, 0g total fat, 0g sat fat, 0mg cholesterol, 0mg sodium, 34g carbohydrate, 0g fiber, 0g protein*

Cindy Loomis, Rushville, NY

Maple-Glazed Frankies

Whenever I make these little treats and put them on an appetizer table, they are the first to disappear!

Makes about 3-1/2 dozen, Serves 14

1 t. butter
1 T. reduced-sodium soy sauce
1/4 c. pure maple syrup
14-oz. pkg. turkey cocktail wieners

In a saucepan over medium-low heat, stir together butter, soy sauce and maple syrup until slightly thickened. Add wieners and heat through.

Nutrition Per Serving: *62 calories, 3g total fat, 1g sat fat, 20mg cholesterol, 304mg sodium, 6g carbohydrate, 0g fiber, 5g protein*

KITCHEN TIP
Keep cocktail wieners in the freezer to have on hand for guests that drop by. They freeze well, cook up quickly and everyone loves them!

Maple-Glazed Frankies

Charlotte Harding, Starkville, MS

Summertime Iced Tea

Add a sprig of fresh mint to each glass for a refreshing touch.

Makes 10 servings

4 c. boiling water
2 family-size tea bags
6 leaves fresh mint
6-oz. can frozen lemonade
   concentrate
1 c. sugar
5 c. cold water
ice cubes
Garnish: fresh mint sprigs

Pour boiling water into a large heatproof pitcher. Add tea bags and mint leaves; let stand for 5 minutes. Discard tea bags and mint leaves. Add frozen lemonade, sugar and cold water, mixing well. Serve over ice; garnish with mint sprigs.

Nutrition Per Serving: *105 calories, 0g total fat, 0g sat fat, 0mg cholesterol, 0mg sodium, 27g carbohydrate, 0g fiber, 0g protein*

Jewel Grindley, Lindenhurst, IL

Seeded Tortilla Crisps

These little strips of crunchiness are so good as an appetizer or with soups or salads.

Serves 12

2 T. butter, melted
8 10-inch flour tortillas
1/2 c. grated Parmesan cheese
1 egg white, beaten
Garnish: sesame, poppy
   and/or caraway seed, onion
   powder, cayenne pepper or
   dried cumin

Brush butter lightly over one side of each tortilla; sprinkle evenly with cheese and press down lightly. Carefully turn tortillas over. Brush other side with egg white and sprinkle with desired seeds and seasoning. Cut each tortilla into 4 strips with a pastry cutter or knife. Place strips cheese-side down on a baking sheet sprayed with non-stick vegetable spray. Bake at 400 degrees, on middle rack of oven, for 8 to 10 minutes, until crisp and golden. Cool on a wire rack.

Nutrition Per Serving: *121 calories, 4g total fat, 2g sat fat, 7mg cholesterol, 250mg sodium, 15g carbohydrate, 0g fiber, 6g protein*

Seeded Tortilla Crisps

Barb Sulser, Delaware, OH

Cheesy Potato Puffs

We can't stop nibbling on these golden little morsels!

Serves 6

4-oz. pkg. instant potato flakes
1/2 c. shredded Cheddar cheese
1/2 c. bacon bits
Optional: paprika

Prepare potato flakes according to package directions; let cool. Stir in cheese; roll into 1-1/2 inch balls. Roll balls in bacon bits; arrange on an ungreased baking sheet. Sprinkle with paprika, if desired. Bake at 375 degrees for 15 to 18 minutes.

Nutrition Per Serving: *110 calories, 7g total fat, 3g sat fat, 16mg cholesterol, 239mg sodium, 6g carbohydrate, 1g fiber, 5g protein*

GOOD TO KNOW
Cheddar cheese can be mild, sharp or extra sharp. Sharp is the term that indicates how Cheddar changes in flavor and texture as it continues to age. As the cheese ages, it goes from mild to tangier with a more complex and deep flavor.

Lisa McClelland, Columbus, OH

Cucumber-Lime Agua Fresca

On a trip to Mexico, I was served this beverage one hot day. It's very refreshing...a great way to use up cucumbers and mint! The lime adds the tartness.

Makes 4 servings

1 lb. cucumbers, cubed
6 c. water, divided
1/4 c. fresh mint, chopped
2 T. sugar
2 T. lime juice
ice cubes
Garnish: lime slices, cucumber
   slices

Combine cucumbers, 2 cups water and mint in a blender. Process until puréed. Let stand in blender for 5 minutes to steep. Strain purée into a 2-quart pitcher. Add remaining water, sugar, lime juice and ice. Stir to combine; add more sugar, if desired. Divide evenly into 4 tall glasses; garnish as desired. Serve immediately.

Nutrition Per Serving: *42 calories, 0g total fat, 0g sat fat, 0mg cholesterol, 4mg sodium, 10g carbohydrate, 1g fiber, 1g protein*

Cucumber-Lime Agua Fresca

Jackie Smulski, Lyons, IL

Apple Wheels

So simple to make and so yummy to eat...the kids will love them!

Makes 12 servings

1/4 c. reduced-fat creamy peanut
   butter
2 t. honey
1/4 c. semi-sweet mini chocolate
   chips
1 T. raisins
4 red or yellow apples, cored

Combine peanut butter and honey in a bowl; fold in chocolate chips and raisins. Fill centers of apples with mixture; refrigerate for one hour. Slice apples into 1/4-inch rings to serve.

Nutrition Per Serving: *93 calories, 4g total fat, 1g sat fat, 0mg cholesterol, 26mg sodium, 15g carbohydrate, 2g fiber, 2g protein*

Kris Axtell, Johnson City, TX

Presto Pesto

Everyone loves pesto and this one is so easy to make! You'll want to keep it on hand for sandwiches, soups and scrambled eggs.

Serves 8

2-1/2 c. fresh basil, chopped
   and packed
1/4 c. pine nuts or walnuts, chopped
1/2 c. grated Parmesan cheese
2 cloves garlic, minced
1/4 c. olive oil
1/4 t. salt
1/4 t. pepper

Add basil, pine nuts or walnuts to the food processor and pulse until well blended. Add cheese and garlic and pulse several times more, scraping down the sides. While the food processor is running, slowly add olive oil in a steady small stream. Occasionally, stop to scrape down the sides of the food processor. Add salt and pepper to taste. Store in refrigerator until ready to use, or freeze in small containers to use later.

Nutrition Per Serving: *118 calories, 12g total fat, 2g sat fat, 5mg cholesterol, 169mg sodium, 1g carbohydrate, 0g fiber, 3g protein*

Presto Pesto

Sharon Taylor, Angelica, NY

4-Layer Mexican Dip

Guests will welcome fresh and healthy veggie dippers such as baby carrots, celery stalks and broccoli flowerets as well as crispy crackers.

Serves 8

8-oz. pkg. low-fat cream cheese, softened
15-oz. can chili with beans
16-oz. jar salsa
8-oz. pkg. shredded Mexican-blend cheese
tortilla chips or crackers

Spread cream cheese into the bottom of an ungreased, microwave-safe 11"x7" glass baking pan. Layer chili, salsa and cheese on top. Microwave on high for 5 to 7 minutes, until hot and bubbly and cheeses are melted. Serve warm with tortilla chips or crackers for dipping.

Nutrition Per Serving: *214 calories, 13g total fat, 7g sat fat, 41mg cholesterol, 864mg sodium, 13g carbohydrate, 3g fiber, 13g protein*

Ellie Brandel, Milwaukie, OR

Cranberry-Lime Cooler

This lime cooler is so pretty and refreshing with the tangy cranberry juice and sprigs of mint.

Makes 8 servings

6-oz. can frozen limeade concentrate, thawed
4 c. cold water
16-oz. bottle cranberry juice cocktail
1/4 c. sugar-free orange drink mix
ice
Garnish: fresh mint sprigs

Prepare limeade with water in a large pitcher. Stir in cranberry juice and orange drink mix. Pour over ice in tall mugs or glasses. Garnish each with a sprig of mint.

Nutrition Per Serving: *73 calories, 0g total fat, 0g sat fat, 0mg cholesterol, 3mg sodium, 19g carbohydrate, 0g fiber, 0g protein*

Cranberry-Lime Cooler

Sandy Benham, Sanborn, NY

Strawberry-Watermelon Slush

This is a luscious combination of fresh summer fruit that everyone always loves!

Makes 6 servings

1 pt. strawberries, hulled and halved
2 c. watermelon, cubed and seeded
1/3 c. sugar
1/3 c. lemon juice
2 c. ice cubes

Combine all ingredients except ice cubes in a blender. Process until smooth. Gradually add ice and continue to blend. Serve immediately.

Nutrition Per Serving: *80 calories, 0g total fat, 0g sat fat, 0mg cholesterol, 1mg sodium, 21g carbohydrate, 1g fiber, 1g protein*

Ann Farris, Biscoe, AR

Prosciutto-Wrapped Asparagus

Fresh asparagus never tasted so good!

Makes 12 servings

2 bunches asparagus, about
   24 pieces, trimmed
1 T. olive oil
1 t. pepper
3-oz. pkg. sliced prosciutto, cut into
   strips with fat removed
Optional: lemon slices

Toss asparagus with oil and pepper. Arrange in a single layer on an ungreased rimmed baking sheet. Bake at 400 degrees for 5 minutes. Allow to cool slightly. Wrap each asparagus spear with a strip of prosciutto. Return to oven and bake for 4 more minutes, or until asparagus is crisp-tender and prosciutto is slightly browned. Serve warm or at room temperature, garnished with lemon slices if desired.

Nutrition Per Serving: *34 calories, 2g fat, 0g sat fat, 7mg cholesterol, 166mg sodium, 2g carbohydrate, 1g fiber, 3g protein*

Prosciutto-Wrapped Asparagus

Regina Kostyu, Delaware, OH

Special Deviled Eggs

These deviled eggs will become your favorites with the hint of spice in the coleslaw dressing.

Makes 2 dozen, serves 12

1 doz. eggs, hard-boiled and peeled
3 to 4 T. reduced-fat coleslaw
    dressing
1/8 to 1/4 t. garlic salt with parsley
Garnish: paprika, snipped fresh
    chives

Slice eggs in half lengthwise; scoop yolks into a bowl. Arrange whites on a serving platter; set aside. Mash yolks well with a fork. Stir in dressing to desired consistency and add garlic salt to taste. Spoon or pipe yolk mixture into whites. Garnish as desired; chill.

Nutrition Per Serving: *79 calories, 5g total fat, 2g sat fat, 217mg cholesterol, 146mg sodium, 3g carbohydrate, 0g fiber, 6g protein*

Heather Rogers, Dayton, OH

Simple Tomato Bruschetta

This bruschetta is fun to serve because each person puts the topping on the crusty bread themselves. Toast a variety of breads and arrange then on a long cutting board to serve.

Serves 6

4 to 5 plum tomatoes, chopped
1/4 c. red onion, diced
1 clove garlic, minced
1 T. olive oil
1 t. dried oregano
1 whole-grain baguette, sliced and
    toasted

Place tomatoes in a large bowl with a lid. Add onion, garlic, oil and oregano; toss to mix. Cover and refrigerate for 30 minutes to allow flavors to blend. To serve, spoon onto toasted baguette slices.

Nutrition Per Serving: *94 calories, 3g total fat, 0g sat fat, 0mg cholesterol, 122mg sodium, 14g carbohydrate, 3g fiber, 5g protein*

Simple Tomato Bruschetta

Rita Barnett, Lewisburg, TN

Texas Hominy

I got this recipe from my aunt, who lived in Texas for several years while her husband was stationed there in the Air Force. When my son's school cafeteria asked for recipes to serve to the students, this turned out to be quite popular. My teenage son has often eaten at least half of it in one sitting!

Serves 8

15-1/2 oz. can hominy, drained
15-oz. can chili
2 c. tortilla or corn chips, crushed
1-1/2 to 2 c. shredded Cheddar or
    Mexican-blend cheese

In a lightly greased 9"x9" baking pan, combine hominy and chili, stirring well. Top with chips and cheese. Bake, uncovered, at 350 degrees for 25 to 30 minutes, until heated through and cheese melts.

Nutrition Per Serving: *184 calories, 8g total fat, 2g sat fat, 13mg cholesterol, 475mg sodium, 24g carbohydrate, 4g fiber, 6g protein*

Anna McMaster, Portland, OR

Cucumber & Salmon Slices

The rich salmon mixture also makes a great sandwich spread.

Makes about 48, serves 12

3-oz. cooked salmon fillet
1 t. lemon juice
1 t. fresh dill, chopped
1/2 c. plain Greek yogurt
3 whole cucumbers
Garnish: fresh dill or parsley sprigs

Blend salmon, lemon juice, dill and yogurt. Place in a covered container and chill one hour. Make a design on the outside of the whole cucumbers by slicing several thin strips of peel from the length of the cucumber, or scoring the peel with the tines of a fork. Cut into 1/2-inch slices. Spread with chilled salmon mixture and garnish with dill or parsley.

Nutrition Per Serving: *32 calories, 1g fat, 0g sat fat, 4mg cholesterol, 14mg sodium, 4g carbohydrate, 0g fiber, 3g protein*

Cucumber & Salmon Slices

Mary Hastings, Gurnee, IL

Reuben Bread-Bowl Dip

All the taste of the classic sandwich is in this cheesy dip.

Serves 12

2 16-oz. round loaves rye bread
8-oz. pkg. low-fat cream cheese, softened
1 c. shredded mozzarella cheese
2 2-1/2 oz. pkgs. dried, chipped beef, diced

Hollow out the center of one loaf of bread; set aside. Cube removed rye bread and remaining loaf; set aside. Mix cheeses together; fold in chipped beef. Spoon into center of bread bowl; bake on a baking sheet at 350 degrees for 1-1/4 hours.
Serve warm on a serving platter surrounded with bread cubes.

Nutrition Per Serving: *276 calories, 8g total fat, 4g sat fat, 27mg cholesterol, 965mg sodium, 38g carbohydrate, 4g fiber, 14g protein*

Mary Bruhn, Newton, IA

Traditional Hummus

Hummus has become a staple in our home because it is so good as a snack or to accompany almost any meat.

Makes 3 cups, serves 12

2 c. canned garbanzo beans, rinsed and drained
2 cloves garlic, finely minced
1/2 t. salt
1/2 t. pepper
2 T. lime juice
1 T. tahini
1 T. olive oil
1/2 to 1 c. no-salt tomato juice
Garnish: red pepper flakes, chopped parsley
toasted pita chips

Place garbanzo beans in a food processor. Cover and process until blended. Add garlic, salt and pepper. Cover and process until combined. Add lime juice, tahini and olive oil. Cover and process until well blended. Mixture will be thick. With machine running, slowly add enough tomato juice to make mixture the desired consistency. Transfer to a serving bowl. If desired, garnish red pepper flakes and chopped parsley. Serve with toasted pita chips.

Nutrition Per Serving: *69 calories, 2g total fat, 0g sat fat, 0mg cholesterol, 220mg sodium, 10g carbohydrate, 2g fiber, 2g protein*

KITCHEN TIP
Hummus is fun to make because it can be flavored in so many different ways. Try onion powder, dried basil, dried oregano or chopped fresh dill. Or stir in some minced black olives, sliced green onion or chopped fresh tomato.

Traditional Hummus

Nola Coons, Gooseberry Patch

Honey Garlic Chicken Wings

Yum...these wings really get the party started! Use a disposable plastic slow-cooker liner, and you won't need to scrub the crock. Or cook in your electric pressure cooker on Slow Cook for the same yummy results.

Makes 10 servings

3 lbs. chicken wings
salt and pepper to taste
1 c. honey
1/2 c. soy sauce
2 T. catsup
2 T. oil
1/2 c. water

Sprinkle chicken wings with salt and pepper; place in a slow cooker and set aside. In a bowl, combine remaining ingredients and mix well. Cover and cook on low setting for 6 to 8 hours. If using an electric pressure cooker for this recipe, secure lid and turn pressure release lever to Venting. Press the Slow Cook setting and set temperature as needed for medium.

Nutrition Per Serving: *435 calories, 24g total fat, 6g sat fat, 103mg cholesterol, 525mg sodium, 30g carbohydrate, 0g fiber, 25g protein*

Vickie, Gooseberry Patch

Pink Party Lemonade

This drink is so pretty and tastes so refreshing. Add a mint leaf to the ice cube tray along with the cherry for some extra color and flavor.

Makes 8 servings

6-oz. jar maraschino cherries, drained
12-oz. container frozen pink lemonade concentrate, thawed
1-ltr. bottle sugar-free lemon-lime soda, chilled

Place a cherry in each section of an ice cube tray; fill with water and freeze. Prepare lemonade in a large pitcher, adding water as directed on package. At serving time, stir in soda and serve over prepared ice cubes.

Nutrition Per Serving: *108 calories, 0g total fat, 0g sat fat, 0mg cholesterol, 13mg sodium, 28g carbohydrate, 0g fiber, 0g protein*

KITCHEN TIP
Dressed-up ice cubes can turn a plain drink into a special treat. Try adding curls of lemon rind, dried cranberries or blueberries to traditional or festive-shaped ice cube trays.

Pink Party Lemonade

Susanne Erickson, Columbus, OH

Chinese Chicken Wings

Move over, hot wings. These Asian-inspired chicken wings are packed with flavor and they're baked. Make extra, because the crowd will love them!

Makes 2 to 3 dozen, serves 12

3 lbs. chicken wings
1/2 c. low-sodium soy sauce
1 c. pineapple juice
1/3 c. brown sugar, packed
1 t. ground ginger
1/2 t. pepper
Optional: celery sticks, ranch salad
   dressing

Place wings in a large plastic zipping bag; set aside. Combine soy sauce and next 4 ingredients; pour over wings, turning to coat. Refrigerate overnight, turning several times. Drain wings, discarding marinade; arrange in a single layer on an ungreased jelly-roll pan. Bake at 450 degrees for 25 to 30 minutes, until golden and juices run clear when chicken is pierced with a fork. Serve with celery and ranch dressing, if desired.

Nutrition Per Serving: *288 calories, 18g total fat, 5g sat fat, 86mg cholesterol, 438mg sodium, 10g carbohydrate, 0g fiber, 21g protein*

Rosie Jones, Wabash, IN

Raspberry Punch

For toasting a festive occasion, replace the cider with sparkling white wine.

Makes 8 servings

2 c. apple cider
3 c. cranberry-raspberry juice
   cocktail
1 qt. lemonade
Optional: 1 lemon, thinly sliced,
   fresh mint leaves, fresh
   raspberries

Combine apple cider, cranberry-raspberry juice and lemonade in a large pitcher or punch bowl; chill. If desired, garnish glasses with lemon slices, fresh mint leaves or raspberries.

Nutrition Per Serving: *130 calories, 0g total fat, 0g sat fat, 0mg cholesterol, 9mg sodium, 33g carbohydrate, 0g fiber, 0g protein*

Raspberry Punch

Becca Jones, Jackson, TN

Fabulous Fruit Tea

This fruity tea is perfect for an afternoon party or special event. It serves so many and is easy to make.

Makes 18 servings

12 c. water, divided
1 c. sugar
9 tea bags
12-oz. can frozen lemonade
    concentrate, thawed
12-oz. can frozen orange juice
    concentrate, thawed
3 c. unsweetened pineapple juice
ice

Bring 4 cups water to a boil in a saucepan over high heat. Stir in sugar until dissolved. Remove from heat; add tea bags. Let stand for 8 to 10 minutes to steep; discard tea bags. Pour tea mixture into a large pitcher. Stir in juices and remaining water. Cover and chill; serve over ice.

Nutrition Per Serving: *108 calories, 0g total fat, 0g sat fat, 0mg cholesterol, 1mg sodium, 28g carbohydrate, 0g fiber, 0g protein*

Deanna Smith, Huntington, WV

BLT Bites

A favorite sandwich becomes an appetizer! Use heirloom tomatoes in different colors for a stunning presentation.

Makes 10 servings

20 large cherry tomatoes
4 slices bacon, crisply cooked and
    crumbled
1/2 c. light mayonnaise
1/3 c. green onion, chopped
3 T. grated Parmesan cheese
Optional: 2 T. fresh parsley, finely
    chopped

Cut a thin slice off the top of each tomato; scoop out and discard pulp. Invert tomatoes onto a paper towel to drain. Combine the remaining ingredients in a small bowl; mix well. Spoon mixture into each tomato; refrigerate for several hours before serving.

Nutrition Per Serving: *86 calories, 7g total fat, 2g sat fat, 10mg cholesterol, 206mg sodium, 3g carbohydrate, 1g fiber, 2g protein*

BLT Bites

Helene Hamilton, Hickory, NC

Rosemary Lemon-Pineapple Punch

The fresh rosemary in this drink gives it a unique flavor that makes it savory and sweet.

Makes 12 servings
46-oz. can unsweetened pineapple juice
1-1/2 c. lemon juice
2 c. water
3/4 c. sugar
4 to 5 sprigs fresh rosemary
1-ltr. bottle ginger ale, chilled

In a large saucepan, combine pineapple juice, lemon juice, water, sugar and rosemary sprigs. Bring to a boil over medium heat, stirring until sugar dissolves. Remove from heat; cover and let stand for 15 minutes. Discard rosemary; chill. At serving time, add ginger ale; serve immediately.

Nutrition Per Serving: *342 calories, 0g total fat, 0g sat fat, 0mg cholesterol, 33mg sodium, 83g carbohydrate, 1g fiber, 2g protein*

Anne Alesauskas, Minocqua, WI

Avocado Feta Dip

My family doesn't care for tomatoes but we love red peppers. So I just substituted them for the tomatoes in this recipe.

Makes 3 cups, serves 12
2 avocados, halved, pitted and diced
3/4 c. crumbled feta cheese
1 red pepper, diced
1 T. lemon juice
2 t. dill weed
1/4 t. salt
1/4 t. pepper

Combine all ingredients in a serving bowl; mix until well blended.

Nutrition Per Serving: *66 calories, 6g total fat, 2g sat fat, 8mg cholesterol, 156mg sodium, 3g carbohydrate, 2g fiber, 2g protein*

GOOD TO KNOW
Avocados are full of healthy nutrients like potassium, vitamin C and B6. This versatile fruit can be used in salads, sandwiches, and dips, or just eaten alone.

Avocado Feta Dip

Teriyaki Pork Tenderloin, p. 184

CHAPTER SIX

QUICK-TO-FIX
Dinners

Tuna Noodle Casserole, p. 212

Baked Crumbed Haddock, p. 204

Charlene McCain, Bakersfield, CA

Inside-Out Stuffed Pepper

A quick and tasty dish for those nights when you get home late and everybody's hungry...super-simple to toss together and satisfies even the biggest of hungers!

Serves 4

1 green pepper, top removed
1 lb. ground beef
1 onion, chopped
1-1/2 c. cooked rice
8-oz. can tomato sauce
salt and pepper to taste

Bring a saucepan of salted water to a boil. Add green pepper and cook for 8 to 10 minutes, until tender. Drain; cool slightly and chop pepper. Meanwhile, cook beef and onion in a skillet over medium heat, stirring often, until beef is browned and onion is translucent. Drain; add green pepper and cooked rice to skillet. Pour tomato sauce over beef mixture; stir and heat through. Season with salt and pepper to taste.

Nutrition Per Serving: *315 calories, 12g total fat, 5g sat fat, 73mg cholesterol, 83mg sodium, 26g carbohydrate, 2g fiber, 25g protein*

Terri Lock, Carrollton, MO

Beef Porcupine Meatballs

As a teacher, I need fast homestyle meals to serve to my family of five before I leave for evening school events...this recipe is perfect.

Serves 6

8-oz. pkg. beef-flavored rice
  vermicelli mix
1 lb. ground beef
1 egg, beaten
2-1/2 c. water
cooked egg noodles

In a bowl, combine rice vermicelli mix, beef and egg, reserving seasoning packet from mix. Form mixture into one-inch balls. In a skillet over medium heat, cook meatballs, turning occasionally, until browned on all sides; drain. In a bowl, combine seasoning packet and water; pour over meatballs. Cover and simmer for 30 minutes, or until thickened and meatballs are no longer pink in the center. Serve meatballs and sauce over noodles.

Nutrition Per Serving: *303 calories, 8g total fat, 3g sat fat, 84mg cholesterol, 669mg sodium, 36g carbohydrate, 1g fiber, 20g protein*

Beef Porcupine Meatballs

Pam Colden, Brodhead, WI

Scalloped Potatoes & Ham

Everyone loves this comfort food dish. The soup in this recipe makes it so rich and creamy.

Serves 6

8 potatoes, peeled and sliced
1 c. cooked ham, diced
1 small onion, diced
1/2 c. low-fat shredded Cheddar
   cheese
salt and pepper to taste
10-3/4 oz. can low-salt cream of
   chicken soup

In a slow cooker, layer each ingredient in the order given, spreading soup over top. Do not stir. Cover and cook on low setting for 8 to 10 hours, or on high setting for 5 hours.

Nutrition Per Serving: *316 calories, 3g total fat, 1g sat fat, 18mg cholesterol, 575mg sodium, 58g carbohydrate, 4g fiber, 15g protein*

Cherylann Smith, Efland, NC

Herb & Garlic Shrimp

This shrimp dish is often requested by my children....and when Daddy isn't looking, they sneak shrimp off his plate!

Makes 4 to 6 servings

1 clove garlic, pressed
2 T. olive oil
6 T. butter, sliced
1 lb. fresh shrimp or frozen cooked
   shrimp, tails on
1.8-oz. pkg. savory herb with garlic
   soup mix
1 c. warm water

In a skillet over medium heat, sauté garlic in olive oil and butter for 2 minutes. Add shrimp and simmer until shrimp is cooked or thawed, stirring often. Dissolve soup mix in water; pour over shrimp mixture. Reduce heat; simmer until heated through, about 20 minutes.

Nutrition Per Serving: *243 calories, 17g total fat, 8g sat fat, 144mg cholesterol, 712mg sodium, 7g carbohydrate, 0g fiber, 15g protein*

Herb & Garlic Shrimp

Vickie, Gooseberry Patch

Peppered Beef in Parsley Crust

This is an elegant recipe but so simple to make. Everyone is always so impressed with this lovely dish.

Serves 6

2 T. whole peppercorns
4 T. butter, softened
1 c. fresh parsley, chopped
2-lb. beef tenderloin roast

Grind peppercorns until coarse in texture and spread evenly on a large platter. Blend together butter and parsley in a small bowl. Spread butter mixture over roast, covering all sides evenly. Place roast on platter and roll in cracked peppercorns until roast is coated. Place roast in a shallow roasting pan. Bake at 425 degrees for one hour, or until meat thermometer registers 135 degrees; this will produce a rare roast. Let rest before carving.

Nutrition Per Serving: *444 calories, 35g total fat, 16g sat fat, 120mg cholesterol, 82mg sodium, 1g carbohydrate, 0g fiber, 30g protein*

Brenda Rogers, Atwood, CA

South-of-the-Border Squash Skillet

Our family grows lots of yellow summer squash in our community garden. We love tacos, so this taco-flavored recipe is a yummy way to use it up! If you omit the meat, it's also a great vegetarian dish.

Makes 4 servings

1 lb. ground beef or turkey
1/3 c. onion, diced
1 c. water
1-1/4 oz. pkg. taco seasoning mix
4 to 5 yellow squash, zucchini or
    crookneck squash, chopped
1 c. shredded Cheddar cheese

In a skillet over medium heat, brown meat with onion; drain. Stir in water and taco seasoning; add squash. Cover and simmer for about 10 minutes, until squash is tender. Stir in cheese; cover and let stand just until cheese melts.

Nutrition Per Serving: *368 calories, 21g total fat, 11g sat fat, 102mg cholesterol, 960mg sodium, 14g carbohydrate, 4g fiber, 32g protein*

South-of-the-Border Squash Skillet

Ginny Bone, St. Peters, MO

BBQ Chicken Pizza

This yummy pizza makes a super-fast & easy dinner any night of the week.

Serves 4

12-inch Italian pizza crust
3 c. cooked chicken, shredded
1 c. low-sodium barbecue sauce
1/2 c. shredded low-sodium
   mozzarella cheese
1/2 c. shredded low-sodium Cheddar
   cheese

Place pizza crust on a lightly greased 12" round pizza pan. Combine chicken and barbecue sauce; spread on pizza crust. Sprinkle with cheeses. Bake at 450 degrees for 8 to 10 minutes, or until cheeses melt and crust is crisp.

Nutrition Per Serving: *565 calories, 14g total fat, 5g sat fat, 81mg cholesterol, 801mg sodium, 65g carbohydrate, 1g fiber, 39g protein*

Brita Greenough, Ankeny, IA

Teriyaki Pork Tenderloin

We love to serve this with grilled or warmed pineapple slices and rice. It makes a very pretty and filling meal.

Serves 8

2 pork tenderloins, about 1 lb. each,
   cut in half
1 t. pepper
2 T. olive oil
1 T. green onion, sliced
2 c. teriyaki sauce
Garnish: sliced green onions,
   sesame seed

Rub all sides of tenderloins with pepper. In a skillet, sear tenderloins in oil about 3 minutes on each side, or until nicely browned. Add green onion and teriyaki sauce; cook for 3 minutes. Place tenderloins and sauce in a greased 13"x9" baking pan and cover with foil. Bake at 350 degrees for about one hour until meat tests 160 degrees on a meat thermometer. Let meat rest for 5 to 8 minutes before slicing. Slice tenderloins and serve on a platter, drizzled with sauce and garnished with sesame seed and green onions if desired.

Nutrition Per Serving: *216 calories, 6g total fat, 1g sat fat, 73mg cholesterol, 1964mg sodium, 11g carbohydrate, 0g fiber, 28g protein*

Teriyaki Pork Tenderloin

Sheryl Eastman, Wixom, MI

Sausage & Apple Kraut

Serve with mashed potatoes, buttered green beans and fresh-baked bread for a chilly-weather meal.

Makes 4 to 6 servings

27-oz. jar sauerkraut, drained, rinsed and divided
1 lb. Kielbasa sausage, sliced and divided
2 tart apples, peeled, cored and diced
1/2 c. brown sugar, packed and divided
2 c. apple cider or juice, divided

In a lightly greased 13"x9" baking pan, layer half of the sauerkraut, half of the sausage and all the apples. Sprinkle with 1/4 cup brown sugar. Pour one cup cider or juice over top. Repeat layering. Cover and bake at 350 degrees for 1-1/2 hours, or until sauerkraut is caramelized and golden.

Nutrition Per Serving: *330 calories, 13g total fat, 5g sat fat, 52mg cholesterol, 1292mg sodium, 43g carbohydrate, 4g fiber, 11g protein*

Bonnie Yeska, Hinsdale, MT

Salmon Patties

This traditional comfort food dinner is easy to make and fries up in minutes!

Makes 4 servings

14-3/4 oz. can salmon, drained and 2 T. liquid reserved
1 egg, beaten
1/3 c. onion, minced
1/4 c. all-purpose flour
2 t. baking powder
2 T. canola oil
salt and pepper to taste

Combine salmon, egg, onion and flour in a medium bowl; set aside. In a small bowl, mix together reserved salmon liquid and baking powder; stir into salmon mixture. Form into 4 patties. Heat oil in a large skillet over medium heat; add patties. Cook until golden on both sides. Sprinkle with salt and pepper.

Nutrition Per Serving: *264 calories, 17g total fat, 3g sat fat, 125mg cholesterol, 735mg sodium, 6g carbohydrate, 0g fiber, 24g protein*

Salmon Patties

Angela Couillard, Lakeville, MN

Sausage-Stuffed Squash

These are so inviting on each individual plate. The smoky flavor of the turkey sausage combines with the sweet brown sugar for that perfect savory, sweet combination. Everyone always loves them!

Makes 4 servings

12-oz. pkg. smoked turkey sausage, diced
1/4 c. dark brown sugar, packed
1/4 t. dried sage
2 acorn squash, halved and seeded
1 c. water

In a bowl, mix together sausage, brown sugar and sage; toss to mix well. Fill squash halves heaping full with sausage mixture; wrap each stuffed half with aluminum foil. Pour water into a large slow cooker; place wrapped squash halves in slow cooker, stacking if necessary. Cover and cook on low setting for 6 to 8 hours.

Nutrition Per Serving: *271 calories, 8g total fat, 0g sat fat, 45mg cholesterol, 790mg sodium, 40g carbohydrate, 4g fiber, 14g protein*

Cari Simons, Lawrence, KS

Italian Mini Meatloaves

The cheese on these little meatloaves makes them even yummier!

Makes 6 servings

1 lb. ground beef
16-oz. pkg. stuffing mix
1/2 c. water
1 egg, beaten
1 t. Italian seasoning
1 c. tomato-basil pasta sauce
3/4 c. shredded mozzarella cheese

Mix beef, stuffing mix, water, egg and seasoning together until well blended. Spray a muffin tin with non-stick vegetable spray. Press mixture evenly into 12 muffin cups. Make a small well in the center of each; spoon some sauce into each well. Bake, uncovered, at 375 degrees for about 30 minutes, until cooked through. Sprinkle with cheese and bake for 5 to 7 more minutes, until cheese is melted.

Nutrition Per Serving: *504 calories, 15g total fat, 6g sat fat, 96mg cholesterol, 1516mg sodium, 62g carbohydrate, 4g fiber, 28g protein*

Italian Mini Meatloaves

Lisa Arning, Garden City, NY

Poppy's Onion Pizza

For a light vegetarian dinner, this pizza is the best choice.

Serves 8

3 T. olive oil, divided
10-inch refrigerated pizza crust
2 onions, diced
garlic powder to taste
paprika to taste
Optional: salt and pepper to taste

Lightly coat pizza pan with one tablespoon olive oil; place pizza dough into pan. Coat dough with one tablespoon olive oil; set aside. Sauté onions in remaining olive oil until golden; spread evenly over the pizza dough, lightly pressing down. Sprinkle with garlic powder and paprika; add salt and pepper, if desired. Bake at 425 degrees for 20 minutes or until golden.

Nutrition Per Serving: *164 calories, 8g total fat, 1g sat fat, 0mg cholesterol, 260mg sodium, 20g carbohydrate, 2g fiber, 6g protein*

Rick Pasternack, Ipswich, MA

Bacon Florentine Fettuccine

This is a beautiful dish and so easy to make. I keep frozen spinach on hand so I can make this any night of the week.

Serves 4

16-oz. pkg. fettuccine, uncooked
2 10-oz. pkgs. frozen creamed spinach
1/2 lb. bacon, crisply cooked and crumbled
1/8 t. garlic powder
1/2 c. plus 2 T. grated Parmesan cheese, divided
pepper to taste

Prepare fettuccine as directed on package; drain, reserving 3/4 cup of cooking liquid. Return fettuccine and reserved liquid to saucepan. Microwave spinach as directed on package. Add spinach, bacon and garlic powder to saucepan; mix well. Transfer to a serving dish; stir in 1/2 cup Parmesan cheese. Add pepper to taste; sprinkle with remaining cheese.

Nutrition Per Serving: *842 calories, 32g total fat, 12g sat fat, 81mg cholesterol, 1542mg sodium, 93g carbohydrate, 6g fiber, 44g protein*

Bacon Florentine Fettuccine

Amy Nicol, Marysville, OH

Steak & Spinach Pinwheel

Such a stunning presentation for special occasions.

Serves 6

1-1/4 lbs. beef flank steak or top
    round steak, halved lengthwise
3/4 t. lemon-pepper seasoning
1/4 t. salt
8 slices bacon, partially cooked
10-oz. pkg. frozen chopped spinach,
    thawed, drained and pressed dry
2 T. dry bread crumbs
1/2 t. dried thyme

With a sharp knife, score both pieces of steak in a diamond pattern with cuts one-inch apart. Repeat on other side. Place one piece of steak between 2 lengths of wax paper; pound lightly into a 10-inch by 6-inch rectangle. Repeat with second piece. Blend seasoning and salt; sprinkle each steak evenly with half of mixture. Arrange 4 slices of bacon lengthwise on each. Combine remaining ingredients in a bowl; spread half of spinach mixture over each steak. Starting at a short end, roll up each steak. Place seam-side down on an aluminum foil-lined, lightly greased broiler pan. Broil for 11 to 13 minutes, to desired doneness. Let stand for 2 to 3 minutes before slicing.

Nutrition Per Serving: *226 calories, 12g total fat, 4g sat fat, 44mg cholesterol, 523mg sodium, 4g carbohydrate, 2g fiber, 26g protein*

Cecilia Ollivares, Santa Paula, CA

Curried Chicken with Mango

We love this meal for a change of pace in the middle of the week. And if you are lactose intolerant you will love this creamy dairy-free dish.

Serves 6

2 T. oil
4 boneless, skinless chicken breasts,
    cooked and sliced
13.6-oz. can coconut milk
1 c. mango, peeled, pitted and cubed
2 to 3 T. curry powder
cooked jasmine rice

Heat oil in a large skillet over medium heat. Cook chicken in oil until golden and warmed through. Stir in milk, mango and curry powder. Simmer for 10 minutes, stirring occasionally, or until slightly thickened. Serve over rice.

Nutrition Per Serving: *384 calories, 29g total fat, 16g sat fat, 72mg cholesterol, 81mg sodium, 8g carbohydrate, 2g fiber, 25g protein*

Curried Chicken with Mango

Erin Tingle, Ephrata, PA

Easy Italian Chicken with Pasta

This is my go-to dish for those busy game nights. It fills everyone up and is so tasty.

Serves 4

4 boneless, skinless chicken breasts
1/4 c. grated Parmesan cheese, divided
2 T. Italian seasoning, divided
Optional: 2 T. garlic powder, divided
6-oz. pkg. angel hair pasta, cooked
26-oz. jar spaghetti sauce, heated

Place chicken breasts in a broiler pan; sprinkle with half of the cheese, half of the Italian seasoning and half of the garlic powder if using. Broil for 5 to 10 minutes; turn chicken breasts and sprinkle with remaining cheese, Italian seasoning and garlic powder if using. Broil for an additional 5 to 10 minutes or until juices run clear when pierced with a fork. Serve chicken over top of pasta and pour sauce over all.

Nutrition Per Serving: *630 calories, 23g total fat, 7g sat fat, 117mg cholesterol, 950mg sodium, 57g carbohydrate, 6g fiber, 46g protein*

Claire Bertram, Lexington, KY

Greek Tilapia with Orzo

If you like tilapia, you will want to serve this dish often. Because the fish is so mild, you'll love that the oregano and lemon perk it right up!

Serves 4

1-1/2 lbs. tilapia fillets, thawed if frozen
juice and zest of 1 lemon
1 T. fresh oregano, snipped
salt and pepper to taste
1 pt. cherry tomatoes, halved
8-oz. pkg. orzo pasta, cooked

Rinse fish fillets and pat dry. Place in a lightly greased 13"x9" baking pan. Sprinkle fish evenly with lemon juice and zest, oregano, salt and pepper. Arrange tomatoes around fish; cover with aluminum foil. Bake at 400 degrees for 16 to 18 minutes, until fish is opaque and tomatoes are tender. Serve over cooked orzo, drizzled with juices from baking pan.

Nutrition Per Serving: *385 calories, 4g total fat, 2g sat fat, 84mg cholesterol, 95mg sodium, 46g carbohydrate, 3g fiber, 42g protein*

Greek Tilapia with Orzo

Katherine Murnane, Plattsburgh, NY

Foil-Wrapped Baked Salmon

Short on time? Just wrap up dinner and put it in the oven...you'll have a healthy meal in a jiffy!

Serves 4

4 salmon fillets
1 onion, sliced
1/4 c. butter, diced
1 lemon, thinly sliced
1/4 c. brown sugar, packed

Place each fillet on a piece of aluminum foil that has been sprayed with non-stick vegetable spray. Top fillets evenly with onion slices, diced butter, lemon slices and brown sugar. Fold over foil tightly to make packets; make several holes in top of packets with a fork to allow steam to escape. Arrange packets on an ungreased baking sheet. Bake at 375 degrees for 15 to 20 minutes.

Nutrition Per Serving: *491 calories, 26g total fat, 9g sat fat, 173mg cholesterol, 177mg sodium, 15g carbohydrate, 1g fiber, 46g protein*

Stacie Avner, Delaware, OH

Dijon Chicken with Herbs

This is an easy-to-make dish I serve to family & friends when I want a special evening meal.

Serves 6

6 boneless, skinless chicken breasts
1 t. kosher salt
1 t. pepper
3 T. Dijon mustard
2 T. fresh rosemary, minced
2 T. fresh thyme, minced
2 T. fresh parsley, minced

Sprinkle chicken with salt and pepper. Grill over medium-high heat 5 to 6 minutes per side, or until juices run clear. Remove from grill and brush both sides with mustard; sprinkle with herbs.

Nutrition Per Serving: *147 calories, 3g total fat, 0g sat fat, 80mg cholesterol, 570mg sodium, 2g carbohydrate, 0g fiber, 26g protein*

Dijon Chicken with Herbs

Michelle Schuberg, Big Rapids, MI

White Chicken Pizza

A quick & easy dinner even your most picky eater will love!

Serves 8

13.8-oz. can refrigerated pizza crust
    dough
1 T. olive oil
2 boneless, skinless chicken breasts,
    cubed
Optional: 2 T. garlic, minced
16-oz. jar Alfredo pasta sauce
1/2 c. onion, chopped
8-oz. pkg. shredded mozzarella,
    Parmesan & Romano cheese blend

Spread dough onto a lightly greased pizza baking pan; bake at 425 degrees for 7 minutes. Heat oil in a skillet over medium heat; sauté chicken and garlic, if using, in oil until juices run clear when chicken is pierced. Pour Alfredo sauce over baked crust; sprinkle with chicken and onion. Bake 10 more minutes; top with cheese blend and return to oven until cheeses melt.

Nutrition Per Serving: *336 calories, 16g total fat, 8g sat fat, 73mg cholesterol, 810mg sodium, 24g carbohydrate, 1g fiber, 18g protein*

Jason Keller, Carrollton, GA

Quick & Easy Spareribs

Just add coleslaw and a pot of baked beans for a fantastic picnic meal.

Serves 4 to 6

3-lb. rack pork spareribs, skin
    removed, cut into 2-rib serving-
    size portions
salt and pepper to taste
1 to 2 T. olive oil
1 onion, thickly sliced
1 c. water
1 c. favorite barbecue sauce

Season ribs with salt and pepper. In a large skillet, brown ribs in oil on both sides, about 5 minutes. Transfer browned ribs to a plate. Add onion to drippings in skillet and cook until soft, about 3 minutes. Place ribs and onions in slow cooker. Add water and barbecue sauce. Cover and cook on low setting for 6 to 8 hours, until ribs are falling-apart tender. Transfer ribs to a serving platter; skim fat from sauce and spoon over ribs.

Nutrition Per Serving: *523 calories, 30g total fat, 10g sat fat, 166mg cholesterol, 608mg sodium, 17g carbohydrate, 1g fiber, 44g protein*

Quick & Easy Spareribs

Mary Gage, Wakewood, CA

Italian Orange Roughy

Once marinated, this microwave dinner is ready in under 10 minutes!

Serves 4

1 lb. orange roughy fillets
1/2 c. tomato juice
2 T. white vinegar
.7-oz. pkg. Italian salad dressing mix
1/4 c. green onions, chopped
Optional: 1/4 c. green pepper, chopped

Place fish fillets in a shallow 2-quart microwave-safe dish. Combine tomato juice, vinegar and salad dressing mix. Pour over fish. Cover and refrigerate for 30 minutes. Uncover; sprinkle with onions and pepper if using. Microwave, covered, on high for 3 minutes. Turn fish, cover again and cook 2 to 4 minutes longer, until fish flakes easily. Let cooked fish stand for 2 minutes before uncovering.

Nutrition Per Serving: *97 calories, 1g total fat, 0g sat fat, 68mg cholesterol, 165mg sodium, 2g carbohydrate, 1g fiber, 19g protein*

Jennifer Oglesby, Brookville, IN

Garden-Fresh Pesto Pizza

With this easy pizza, you can really taste what fresh is all about! I came up with this recipe one year when I had a bounty of cherry tomatoes and fresh basil.

Makes 8 servings

1 ready-to-use rectangular pizza crust
1/3 c. basil pesto
1/2 c. shredded mozzarella cheese
1-1/2 c. cherry tomatoes, halved
Optional: 4 leaves fresh basil

Place crust on sheet pan, lightly greased with non-stick vegetable spray if directed on package. Spread pesto over pizza crust and top with cheese. Scatter tomatoes over cheese; add a basil leaf to each quarter of the pizza, if desired. Bake at 425 degrees for about 8 to 10 minutes, until crust is crisp and cheese is lightly golden. Cut into wedges or squares.

Nutrition Per Serving: *240 calories, 13g total fat, 3g sat fat, 6mg cholesterol, 513mg sodium, 25g carbohydrate, 1g fiber, 5g protein*

Garden-Fresh Pesto Pizza

Mary Gage, Wakewood, CA

Italian Sausage Skillet

We like to have this meal on busy nights when we want something easy to make but hearty.

Serves 6

1-1/4 lb. pkg. Italian turkey sausage links
3 zucchini, cubed
1/2 c. onion, chopped
14-1/2 oz. can no-salt stewed tomatoes
3 c. cooked whole-grain pasta

In a skillet over medium heat, cook sausage until no longer pink; drain. Cut sausage into 1/4-inch slices; return to skillet and cook until browned. Add zucchini and onion; cook and stir for 2 minutes. Stir in tomatoes with juice. Reduce heat; cover and simmer for 10 to 15 minutes, until zucchini is tender. Serve mixture over cooked pasta.

Nutrition Per Serving: *341 calories, 10g total fat, 3g sat fat, 65mg cholesterol, 1053mg sodium, 47g carbohydrate, 7g fiber, 23g protein*

Karla Neese, Edmond, OK

Mom's Fall-Apart Sunday Roast

This is the best roast you will ever eat!

Serves 8

3-lb. boneless beef chuck roast
salt, pepper and garlic powder to taste
1 T. canola oil
4 potatoes, peeled and quartered
1 onion, quartered
4 carrots, peeled and cut into chunks
1 lb. fresh green beans, trimmed and halved
1 c. water

Sprinkle roast with salt, pepper and garlic powder to taste. Heat oil in a skillet; brown roast on all sides. Place potatoes in a slow cooker; place roast on top of potatoes. Add onion, carrots and green beans; add water. Cover and cook on low setting for 6 to 8 hours. Remove from cooker and arrange vegetables under the roast to serve.

Nutrition Per Serving: *538 calories, 33g total fat, 13g sat fat, 112mg cholesterol, 134mg sodium, 25g carbohydrate, 4g fiber, 36g protein*

Mom's Fall-Apart Sunday Roast

Rogene Rogers, Bemidji, MN

Pork Chops à la Orange

We love the flavors of pork, oranges and pineapple together!

Serves 8

3 lbs. pork chops
salt and pepper to taste
2 c. orange juice
2 11-oz. cans mandarin oranges, drained
8-oz. can pineapple tidbits, drained
cooked egg noodles

Sprinkle pork chops with salt and pepper; place in a slow cooker. Pour orange juice over pork. Cover and cook on low setting for 6 to 8 hours, or on high setting for 3 to 4 hours. About 30 minutes before serving, add oranges and pineapple; continue cooking just until warm. Serve with cooked noodles.

Nutrition Per Serving: *290 calories, 7g total fat, 2g sat fat, 117mg cholesterol, 103mg sodium, 18g carbohydrate, 1g fiber, 39g protein*

Michelle Waddington, New Bedford, MA

Baked Crumbed Haddock

Delicious! Serve with mac & cheese and steamed broccoli for a down-home dinner.

Serves 8

2 5-1/2 oz. pkgs. onion & garlic croutons
1/4 c. butter, melted
3 lbs. haddock fillets
Optional: lemon slices

Finely grind croutons in a food processor. Toss together croutons and butter. Place fish in a lightly greased 13"x9" baking pan. Sprinkle crouton mixture over fish. Bake, uncovered, at 350 degrees for 20 to 25 minutes, until fish flakes easily with a fork. Top fish with lemon slices, if desired.

Nutrition Per Serving: *358 calories, 14g total fat, 6g sat fat, 110mg cholesterol, 788mg sodium, 25g carbohydrate, 2g fiber 32g protein*

Baked Crumbed Haddock

Gail Blain, Stockton, KS

Ham Steak & Apples Skillet

My grandmother's old black cast-iron skillet brings back wonderful memories of the delicious things she used to make in it. I seek out scrumptious skillet recipes just so I can use Grandma's old skillet...this one is a real family favorite.

Serves 6

3 T. butter
1/2 c. brown sugar, packed
1 T. Dijon mustard
2 c. apples, cored and diced
2 1-lb. bone-in ham steaks

Melt butter in a large skillet over medium heat. Add brown sugar and mustard; bring to a simmer. Add apples; cover and simmer for 5 minutes. Top apples with ham steaks. Cover with a lid; simmer for about 10 more minutes or until apples are tender. Remove ham to a platter and cut into serving-size pieces. Top ham with apples and sauce.

Nutrition Per Serving: *166 calories, 7g total fat, 4g sat fat, 24mg cholesterol, 316mg sodium, 24g carbohydrate, 1g fiber, 4g protein*

Eleanor Dionne, Beverly, MA

Ricotta Gnocchi

This is my mother's recipe from more than forty years ago. She made all her pasta by hand. My children look forward to these each time I make it. Now my daughter has learned how to make these and my grandchildren can't wait to eat them. Very easy to do!

Serves 6

32-oz. container ricotta cheese
1 egg, beaten
1 t. salt
4 c. all-purpose flour, divided
Optional: grated Parmesan cheese, warmed tomato sauce

Combine ricotta, egg and salt in a large bowl; mix thoroughly with a large spoon. Gradually add flour, one cup at a time. When dough is no longer sticky, knead slightly on a lightly floured board. Break off chunks; roll into long ropes. Cut ropes into pieces the size of a cherry. Roll in a little flour with the back of a fork. Place on a clean tea towel to dry. To serve gnocchi, boil for 8 to 10 minutes in a large pot of salted water. Garnish with Parmesan cheese and warmed tomato sauce, if desired.

Nutrition Per Serving: *521 calories, 14g total fat, 8g sat fat, 82mg cholesterol, 588mg sodium, 72g carbohydrate, 2g fiber, 27g protein*

Ricotta Gnocchi

Carolyn Magyar, Ebensburg, PA

Quick Meatballs

Make them ahead...they freeze well.

Serves 8

2 lbs. ground beef
1/4 lb. ground pork sausage
6-oz. pkg. beef-flavored stuffing mix
3 eggs, beaten

Mix all ingredients together; shape into one-inch balls. Arrange on an ungreased baking sheet; bake at 350 degrees for 30 minutes or until done.

Nutrition Per Serving: *347 calories, 18g total fat, 7g sat fat, 163mg cholesterol, 511mg sodium, 16g carbohydrate, 1g fiber, 30g protein*

Tara Horton, Delaware, OH

Chicken Pesto Primavera

One summer I grew basil in my garden and froze batches of homemade pesto in ice cube trays. I made up this recipe to use that yummy pesto. When asparagus isn't in season, I'll toss in some broccoli flowerets...it's just as tasty!

Makes 4 servings

8-oz. pkg. rotini pasta, cooked
2 c. cooked chicken, cubed
1 c. asparagus, steamed and cut into
    1-inch pieces
2 T. basil pesto sauce
1/4 to 1/2 c. chicken broth

Cook pasta according to package directions; drain. In a skillet over medium heat, combine chicken, asparagus, pesto, cooked pasta and 1/4 cup chicken broth. Cook and stir until heated through, adding more broth as needed.

Nutrition Per Serving: *268 calories, 9g total fat, 2g sat fat, 61mg cholesterol, 125mg sodium, 19g carbohydrate, 2g fiber, 27g protein*

Chicken Pesto Primavera

Irene Robinson, Cincinnati, OH

Ham Frittata

My family loves this quick, filling dish for dinner. It's a great way to use up leftover ham.

Serves 2 to 4

1 T. butter
1 c. cooked ham, diced
1/2 c. onion, chopped
1/4 c. green pepper, chopped
4 eggs, beaten
salt and pepper to taste

Melt butter in a microwave-safe bowl; add ham, onion and green pepper. Cover; microwave on high for 2 minutes. Stir in eggs, salt and pepper; microwave on high for an additional 1-1/2 to 2-1/2 minutes. Let stand 3 minutes or until completely set.

Nutrition Per Serving: *163 calories, 11g total fat, 4g sat fat, 238mg cholesterol, 519mg sodium, 4g carbohydrate, 1g fiber, 13g protein*

Shelley Turner, Boise, ID

Homemade Fish Sticks

My kids love these yummy fish sticks! I serve them in diner-style baskets with French fries.

Makes 8 servings

2 lbs. cod fillets
2 eggs
2 T. water
salt and pepper to taste
1-1/2 c. seasoned dry bread crumbs
3 T. grated Parmesan cheese
1/4 c. olive oil
Optional: tartar sauce, lemon
   wedges

Cut fish into 4-inch by one-inch strips; set aside. In a shallow dish, beat together egg, water and seasonings. In a separate dish, mix bread crumbs and cheese. Dip fish into egg mixture; coat with bread crumb mixture and set aside. Heat olive oil in a skillet over medium-high heat. Working in batches, add fish to skillet and cook until flaky and golden, about 3 minutes per side. Drain fish sticks on paper towels. Serve with tartar sauce and lemon wedges, if desired.

Nutrition Per Serving: *264 calories, 11g total fat, 2g sat fat, 103mg cholesterol, 503mg sodium, 16g carbohydrate, 1g fiber, 25g protein*

Homemade Fish Sticks

Jane Moore, Haverford, PA

Crab & Broccoli Rolls

Season these rolls with onion or garlic salt to taste, or spice them up with a dash of hot pepper sauce!

Makes 8 rolls

6-oz. can flaked crabmeat, drained
10-oz. pkg. frozen chopped broccoli, cooked, drained and cooled
1/4 c. mayonnaise
1/2 c. shredded Swiss cheese
8-oz. tube refrigerated crescent rolls, separated

Combine crabmeat, broccoli, mayonnaise and cheese; spread about 2 tablespoons on each crescent. Roll up crescent roll-style; arrange on a lightly greased baking sheet. Bake at 375 degrees for 18 to 20 minutes.

Nutrition Per Serving: *177 calories, 9g total fat, 2g sat fat, 28mg cholesterol, 480mg sodium, 16g carbohydrate, 2g fiber, 9g protein*

Sonna Johnson, Goldfield, IA

Tuna Noodle Casserole

This classic tuna casserole recipe is our family favorite. Serve with fresh fruit for a complete and hearty meal.

Serves 6

16-oz. pkg. wide egg noodles, cooked
10-3/4 oz. can low-sodium cream of mushroom soup
6-oz. can tuna, drained
1 c. frozen peas, thawed
Optional: 4-oz. can sliced mushrooms, drained
1 c. 2% milk
salt and pepper to taste
Optional: 1/2 c. shredded Cheddar cheese

Combine noodles, soup, tuna, peas and mushrooms if using; stir in milk. Add salt and pepper to taste. Spread in a lightly greased 9"x9" baking pan; sprinkle with cheese if using. Bake, uncovered, at 350 degrees for 25 minutes, until hot and bubbly.

Nutrition Per Serving: *389 calories, 6g total fat, 2g sat fat, 80mg cholesterol, 353mg sodium, 62g carbohydrate, 4g fiber, 21g protein*

Tuna Noodle Casserole

Claudia Keller, Carrollton, GA

Haddock & Creamy Dill Sauce

You can grill these fillets or put them under the broiler. Either way they are yummy!

Serves 4

1 lb. haddock fillets
1 T. olive oil
salt and pepper to taste
1/2 c. Greek yogurt
1 T. fresh dill, chopped
1 t. lemon juice
Garnish: fresh dill sprigs, thinly sliced lemon

Brush fish with oil; season with salt and pepper. Place on a lightly oiled grate over medium heat. Grill for about 4 minutes on each side, turning once, until fish flakes easily with a fork. To broil, place seasoned fish on broiler pan. Place under broiler for about 3 minutes on a side until fish flakes easily with a fork. Stir together remaining ingredients except garnish. Serve fillets topped with sauce; garnish as desired.

Nutrition Per Serving: *145 calories, 4g total fat, 1g sat fat, 65mg cholesterol, 100mg sodium, 3g carbohydrate, 0g fiber, 23g protein*

Darlene Nolen, Whittier, NC

Steak San Marco

I found this recipe in our local newspaper over twenty years ago. It has become a favorite of our family.

Serves 4 to 6

1 lb. beef round steak, sliced into thin strips
1 T. oil
1.35-oz. pkg. onion soup mix
28-oz. can diced tomatoes
3 T. cider vinegar
cooked rice

In a skillet over medium heat, brown beef in oil; drain. Add soup mix to beef; mix well. Stir in tomatoes with juice and vinegar. Bring to a low boil and stir until mixed. Reduce heat; cover and simmer for one hour or until beef is tender, stirring occasionally. Serve over cooked rice.

Nutrition Per Serving: *187 calories, 8g total fat, 3g sat fat, 30mg cholesterol, 738mg sodium, 9g carbohydrate, 2g fiber, 18g protein*

Steak San Marco

Cris Goode, Mooresvile, IN

Good & Healthy "Fried" Chicken

We love fried chicken and this recipe is the perfect healthy version.

Makes 5 servings

1 c. whole-grain panko bread crumbs
1 c. cornmeal
2 T. all-purpose flour
salt and pepper to taste
1 c. buttermilk
10 chicken legs

Combine panko, cornmeal, flour, salt and pepper in a gallon-size plastic zipping bag. Coat chicken with buttermilk, one piece at a time. Drop chicken into bag and shake to coat pieces lightly. Arrange chicken on baking pan coated with non-stick vegetable spray. Bake, uncovered, at 350 degrees for 40 to 50 minutes, until chicken juices run clear.

Nutrition Per Serving: *285 calories, 8g total fat, 2g sat fat, 69mg cholesterol, 147mg sodium, 32g carbohydrate, 1g fiber, 21g protein*

Jennifer Niemi, Nova Scotia, Canada

Rosemary Peppers & Fusilli

This colorful, flavorful meatless meal is ready to serve in a jiffy. If you can't find fusilli pasta, try medium shells, rotini or even wagon wheels.

Makes 4 servings

2 to 4 T. olive oil
2 red onions, thinly sliced and
    separated into rings
3 red, orange and/or yellow peppers,
    very thinly sliced
5 to 6 cloves garlic, very thinly sliced
3 t. dried rosemary
salt and pepper to taste
12-oz. pkg. fusilli pasta, cooked
Optional: shredded mozzarella
    cheese

Add oil to a large skillet over medium heat. Add onions to skillet; cover and cook over medium heat for 10 minutes. Stir in remaining ingredients except pasta and cheese; reduce heat. Cook, covered, stirring occasionally, for an additional 20 minutes. Serve vegetable mixture over pasta, topped with cheese if desired.

Nutrition Per Serving: *458 calories, 12g total fat, 2g sat fat, 0mg cholesterol, 12mg sodium, 75g carbohydrate, 6g fiber, 13g protein*

Rosemary Peppers & Fusilli

Brian Johnson, Gastonia, NC

Spicy Sausage & Rice

This spicy sausage dish is quick to make on busy evenings after a long day.

Makes 8 servings

3-1/2 c. cooked rice
16-oz. pkg. smoked sausage links, sliced into bite-size pieces
8-oz. jar salsa
Garnish: diced green pepper, diced tomato, sliced jalapeños

In a large skillet over medium heat, combine all ingredients except garnish. Cook, stirring occasionally, until sausage is heated through and most of the liquid is absorbed. Top servings with diced pepper, diced tomato and jalapeño slices.

Nutrition Per Serving: *272 calories, 16g total fat, 5g sat fat, 34mg cholesterol, 584mg sodium, 22g carbohydrate, 1g fiber, 9g protein*

Michele Molen, Mendon, UT

Simple Baked Mostaccioli

My Italian grandmother always used this quick & easy recipe when she needed a dish for last-minute company or to take to a sick friend.

Serves 5

16-oz. pkg. mostaccioli pasta, uncooked
1 lb. ground beef
salt and pepper to taste
16-oz. jar pasta sauce, divided
8-oz. pkg. shredded mozzarella cheese, divided

Cook pasta according to package directions; drain. Meanwhile, brown beef in a skillet over medium heat. Drain; season with salt and pepper. Ladle a spoonful of pasta sauce into a greased 2-quart casserole dish; add half of cooked pasta. Layer with all of beef mixture, half of remaining sauce and half of cheese; repeat layers with remaining pasta, sauce and cheese. Bake, uncovered, at 375 degrees for about 20 minutes, until hot and bubbly.

Nutrition Per Serving: *689 calories, 22g total fat, 10g sat fat, 94mg cholesterol, 733mg sodium, 79g carbohydrate, 6g fiber, 41g protein*

Simple Baked Mostaccioli

Fresh Fruit Kabobs & Poppy Seed Dip, p. 248

CHAPTER SEVEN

Sweet Treats

Fruity Fresh Sorbet, p. 242

Chocolate Pinwheels, p. 238

Joanne Nagle, Ashtabula, OH

Country-Style Skillet Apples

This is a quick dessert that everyone always loves.

Makes 6 servings

3 T. butter
3 T. sugar
1/2 t. cinnamon
2 T. cornstarch
1 c. water
4 Golden Delicious apples, peeled, cored and sliced

Melt butter in a skillet over medium heat. Stir in sugar, cinnamon and cornstarch; mix well and stir in water. Add apple slices. Cook over medium heat, stirring occasionally, until tender, about 10 minutes.

Nutrition Per Serving: *135 calories, 6g total fat, 4g sat fat, 15mg cholesterol, 1mg sodium, 22g carbohydrate, 3g fiber, 0g protein*

Amy Greenlee, Carterville, IL

Honey-Baked Bananas

My mom shared this recipe for luscious honeyed bananas. They are so quick to make and always a hit!

Serves 6

6 bananas, halved lengthwise
2 T. butter, melted
1/4 c. honey
2 T. lemon juice
Garnish: toasted coconut, lemon slices

Arrange bananas in an ungreased 13"x9" baking pan. Blend remaining ingredients; brush over bananas. Bake, uncovered, at 350 degrees for about 15 minutes, turning occasionally. Garnish with toasted coconut and lemon slices.

Nutrition Per Serving: *182 calories, 4g total fat, 3g sat fat, 10mg cholesterol, 2mg sodium, 39g carbohydrate, 3g fiber, 1g protein*

Honey-Baked Bananas

Barbara Parham Hyde,
Manchester, TN

Stuffed Strawberries

Try using pecans in place of the walnuts for added variety.

Makes 18

20 strawberries, hulled and divided
8-oz. pkg. cream cheese, softened
1/4 c. walnuts, finely chopped
1 T. powdered sugar
Optional: fresh mint leaves

Dice 2 strawberries; set aside. Cut a thin layer from the stem end of the remaining strawberries, forming a base. Starting at opposite end of strawberry, slice into 4 wedges, being careful not to slice through the base; set aside. Beat remaining ingredients together until fluffy; fold in diced strawberries. Spoon 1-1/2 tablespoonfuls into the center of each strawberry. Refrigerate until ready to serve. Garnish with fresh mint leaves, if desired.

Nutrition Per Serving: *61 calories, 5g total fat, 3g sat fat, 14mg cholesterol, 40mg sodium, 3g carbohydrate, 1g fiber, 1g protein*

Judy Lange, Imperial, PA

Ginger Ale Baked Apples

A yummy fall dessert or after-the-game snack!

Serves 4

4 baking apples
1/4 c. golden raisins, divided
4 t. brown sugar, packed and divided
1/2 c. ginger ale

Core apples but do not cut through bottoms. Place apples in an ungreased 8"x8" baking pan. Spoon one tablespoon raisins and one teaspoon brown sugar into center of each apple. Pour ginger ale over apples. Bake, uncovered, at 350 degrees, basting occasionally with ginger ale, for 45 minutes, or until apples are tender. Serve warm or cold.

Nutrition Per Serving: *153 calories, 0g total fat, 0g sat fat, 0mg cholesterol, 7mg sodium, 40g carbohydrate, 5g fiber, 1g protein*

Ginger Ale Baked Apples

Jacklyn Akey, Merrill, WI

Chocolatey Chewy Brownies

You'll love these chewy little squares of chocolate. Cut them into holiday shapes for some extra fun!

Makes about 2 dozen, Serves 24

1 c. butter, softened
2 c. sugar
4 eggs, beaten
1 c. all-purpose flour
4 1-oz. sqs. unsweetened baking
   chocolate, melted
Optional: powdered sugar

In a bowl, beat butter and sugar with an electric mixer on medium speed, until creamy. Beat in eggs, mixing well. Stir in remaining ingredients. Pour into a greased and floured 13"x9" baking pan. Bake at 350 degrees for 30 minutes. Cool. Dust with powdered sugar, if desired. Cut into shapes or squares.

Nutrition Per Serving: *187 calories, 11g total fat, 7g sat fat, 56mg cholesterol, 14mg sodium, 22g carbohydrate, 1g fiber, 2g protein*

Connie Patterson, San Diego, CA

Sautéed Pears

You can use any kind of pears for this dish, but the red ones are so beautiful!

Severs 8

4 red pears
1 T. butter
3 T. brown sugar
1/4 c. dried cranberries
Garnish: pecans

Cut pears in half and remove core. In a skillet, melt butter and add pears. Sauté for about 2 minutes, just until pears begin to soften. Add the brown sugar and cranberries. Cook until tender, about 3 more minutes. Remove to plate and garnish with pecans.

Nutrition Per Serving: *90 calories, 2g total fat, 1g sat fat, 4mg cholesterol, 2mg sodium, 20g carbohydrate, 3g fiber, 0g protein*

Sautéed Pears

Vickie, Gooseberry Patch

Watermelon Fruitsicles

Everyone loves watermelon! This is the perfect pool-party treat.

Makes one dozen

5-lb. watermelon wedge, seeded,
    cubed and divided
1/2 c. sugar
1 env. unflavored gelatin
1 T. lemon juice

Place half of watermelon in a blender; process until smooth. Repeat procedure with remaining watermelon. Strain watermelon purée into a large measuring cup, discarding pulp. Reserve 4 cups watermelon juice. Combine one cup juice and sugar in a saucepan. Sprinkle gelatin over mixture; let stand one minute. Cook over medium heat, stirring constantly, until sugar and gelatin dissolve. Add gelatin mixture to remaining 3 cups watermelon juice; stir in lemon juice and let cool. Pour into 1/3-cup frozen pop molds; freeze.

Nutrition Per Serving: *91 calories, 0g total fat, 0g sat fat, 0mg cholesterol, 3mg sodium, 23g carbohydrate, 1g fiber, 2g protein*

Debbie Blundi, Kunkletown, PA

"Free" Coconut Cookies

I call these my "free" cookies because they are sugar-free, fat-free and dairy-free. Add a teaspoon or two of chopped pecans to the dough, if you like.

Makes 16 cookies, serves 16

8 pitted dates
1 very ripe banana, sliced
1-1/2 c. unsweetened flaked coconut
1/8 t. vanilla extract
1/8 t. pumpkin pie spice

Place dates in a small bowl; add enough water to cover. Let stand for 2 to 4 hours; drain. Place dates, banana, coconut, vanilla and spice in a food processor or blender. Process until smooth and mixture resembles cookie dough. If mixture is too dry, add a drop or 2 of water; if mixture is too sticky, add a little more coconut. Scoop dough by teaspoonfuls onto ungreased baking sheets, one inch apart. Bake at 325 degrees for 10 to 15 minutes, until tips of coconut start to brown on the bottom; cookies will not brown on top. Let cookies stand on baking sheet until cool; remove to a plate. Leave uncovered for the first day, so cookies don't get too moist.

Nutrition Per Serving: *66 calories, 3g total fat, 0g sat fat, 2mg cholesterol, 2mg sodium, 12g carbohydrate, 2g fiber, 1g protein*

"Free" Coconut Cookies

Joyce Stackhouse, Cadiz, OH

Pumpkin Pudding

This recipe is really quick to make and scrumptious...perfect for a light dessert after a big meal. If you are watching your calories, you can use sugar-free pudding mix and skim milk.

Makes 8 servings

2 c. milk
3.4-oz. pkg. instant vanilla pudding
    mix
1 c. canned pumpkin
1 t. vanilla extract
1 t. pumpkin pie spice
1/2 t. cinnamon
Optional: whipped cream

Combine milk and dry pudding mix in a large bowl. Beat with an electric mixer on low speed for one to 2 minutes, until smooth. Add pumpkin, vanilla and spices; mix well. Spoon into individual dessert bowls; cover and chill. If desired, garnish with dollops of whipped cream at serving time.

Nutrition Per Serving: *89 calories, 1g total fat, 1g sat fat, 5mg cholesterol, 205mg sodium, 17g carbohydrate, 1g fiber, 2g protein*

Tina Wright, Atlanta, GA

Simple Skillet Peaches

These peaches are delicious on just about anything you can think of. Cereal, oatmeal, ice cream, cobbler... or use them to top big slices of angel food cake!

Makes about 6 servings

6 c. peaches, peeled, pitted and cut
    into bite-size pieces
1/4 c. sugar
1 T. vanilla extract

Combine peaches and sugar in a large skillet over medium heat. Bring to a boil; reduce heat to medium-low. Simmer until peaches are soft and mixture has thickened, about 20 to 25 minutes. Stir in extract. Serve warm or store in an airtight container in the refrigerator.

Nutrition Per Serving: *92 calories, 0g total fat, 0g sat fat, 0mg cholesterol, 0mg sodium, 24g carbohydrate, 2g fiber, 1g protein*

Simple Skillet Peaches

Holly Curry, Middleburgh, NY

Poppy Seed Cake

This yummy cake slices up beautifully and tastes so good with fresh fruit.

Serves 10

18-1/4 oz. pkg. yellow cake mix
1 c. oil
1 c. Greek yogurt
1/2 c. sugar
4 eggs, beaten
1/4 c. poppy seed

In a large bowl, beat together dry cake mix and all remaining ingredients. Pour into a greased and floured Bundt® pan. Bake at 325 degrees for one hour, or until a toothpick inserted tests clean. Turn cake out onto a serving plate.

Nutrition Per Serving: *524 calories, 32g total fat, 4g sat fat, 86mg cholesterol, 392mg sodium, 54g carbohydrate, 1g fiber, 7g protein*

Tina Knotts, Cable, OH

Quick Sugar Cookies

Everyone needs a dependable sugar cookie recipe...this is mine. I roll them out and cut them in squares when I am in a hurry. So easy!

Makes 4 dozen

2 c. butter, softened
1-1/3 c. sugar
2 eggs, beaten
2 t. vanilla extract
5 c. all-purpose flour

In a large bowl, blend butter and sugar together; stir in eggs and vanilla. Add flour; mix until well blended. Shape dough into a ball; chill in freezer for 10 minutes. Roll out dough 1/4-inch thick on a lightly floured surface. Transfer to parchment paper-lined baking sheet and cut into squares. Or, roll out and cut out with cookie cutters as desired. Bake at 350 degrees for 8 to 10 minutes, until golden. Cool on wire racks.

Nutrition Per Serving: *140calories, 8g total fat, 5g sat fat, 29mg cholesterol, 4mg sodium, 16g carbohydrate, 0g fiber, 2g protein*

Quick Sugar Cookies

Maria Temple, New York, NY

Sugar-Topped Cupcakes

Enjoy these warm cupcakes for a real treat!

Makes 2 dozen, serves 24

18-1/4-oz. pkg. white cake mix
1 c. milk
2 eggs
1/2 t. nutmeg
Optional: 1/3 c. sugar, 1/2 t.
    cinnamon

Blend dry cake mix, milk, eggs and nutmeg at low speed with an electric mixer until just moistened; beat at high speed 2 minutes. Fill paper-lined muffin cups 2/3 full. Bake at 350 degrees until golden, about 15 to 18 minutes. Cool 5 minutes. If desired, combine sugar and cinnamon; sprinkle over cupcakes. Serve warm.

Nutrition Per Serving: *104 calories, 3g total fat, 1g sat fat, 18mg cholesterol, 155mg sodium, 18g carbohydrate, 0g fiber, 2g protein*

Carol Field Dahlstrom, Ankeny, IA

Peach Yogurt Dessert

This dessert was inspired by a peach dessert I had at a friend's house who came from India. I loved the texture and flavor. This is my version of this yummy dessert.

Serves 6

2 c. plain Greek yogurt
1/4 c. powdered sugar
1/4 t. cardamom
2 medium peaches, peeled and pitted
1 t. lemon juice
Garnish: pistachios, sliced peaches

In a large bowl, combine yogurt, sugar and cardamom; set aside. In a blender, purée peaches and lemon juice; stir into yogurt mixture. Refrigerate for at least 2 hours or overnight. To serve, spoon into serving dishes and garnish with pistachios and sliced peaches.

Nutrition Per Serving: *98 calories, 3g total fat, 2g sat fat, 11mg cholesterol, 38mg sodium, 14g carbohydrate, 1g fiber, 5g protein*

Peach Yogurt Dessert

Nancy Willis, Farmington Hills, MI

Easy Apple Crisp

Garnish with a dollop of whipped cream and a dusting of cinnamon or an apple slice for a sweeter treat.

Serves 12

4 c. apples, cored and sliced
1/2 c. brown sugar, packed
1/2 c. quick-cooking oats, uncooked
1/3 c. all-purpose flour
3/4 t. cinnamon
1/4 c. butter
Garnish: whipped cream, cinnamon, apple slice

Arrange apple slices in a greased 11"x8" baking pan; set aside. Combine remaining ingredients; stir until crumbly and sprinkle over apples. Bake at 350 degrees for 30 to 35 minutes. Garnish as desired.

Nutrition Per Serving: *116 calories, 4g total fat, 3g sat fat, 10mg cholesterol, 4mg sodium, 20g carbohydrate, 1g fiber, 1g protein*

Peggy Cummings, Cibolo, TX

Simple Meringues

These beautiful white-as-snow meringues are a sweet, end-of-meal treat.

Makes 3 dozen, Serves 36

2 egg whites
1/8 t. cream of tartar
1/8 t. salt
3/4 c. sugar
1/2 t. vanilla extract

Beat egg whites in a large bowl with an electric mixer at high speed until foamy. Add cream of tartar and salt, beating until mixed; gradually add sugar, one tablespoon at a time, beating well after each addition until stiff peaks form. Stir in vanilla. Drop by teaspoonfuls 1-1/2 inches apart onto greased baking sheets. Bake at 250 degrees for 40 minutes, or until dry. Remove to wire racks to cool completely. Store in an airtight container.

Nutrition Per Serving: *17 calories, 0g total fat, 0g sat fat, 0mg cholesterol, 11mg sodium, 4g carbohydrate, 0g fiber, 0g protein*

Simple Meringues

Marilyn Epley, Stillwater, OK

Honeyed Fruit & Rice

Jasmine rice is also known as fragrant rice and can be found in many markets or specialty stores. With the dried fruit added, it makes a lovely holiday dessert.

Makes 2 servings

2 c. cooked jasmine rice
1/3 c. dried cranberries
1/3 c. dried apricots, chopped
1/4 c. honey
Garnish: milk

Stir together hot cooked rice, cranberries, apricots and honey. Divide into 2 bowls; top with milk.

Nutrition Per Serving: *507 calories, 3g total fat, 2g sat fat, 10mg cholesterol, 56mg sodium, 115g carbohydrate, 3g fiber, 9g protein*

Carole Akers, Bellevue, OH

Butter Pecan Peach Pudding

So refreshing in the summer, or serve warm on chilly days...a yummy treat either way!

Serves 24

29-oz. can sliced peaches in fruit juice
18-1/4 oz. pkg. butter pecan or yellow cake mix
1/2 c. butter, melted
1 c. chopped pecans
1 c. unsweetened flaked coconut

Pour peaches and juice in the bottom of an ungreased 13"x9" baking pan. Cover with dry cake mix; drizzle butter over the top. Sprinkle with pecans and coconut. Bake, uncovered, at 350 degrees for 30 to 35 minutes.

Nutrition Per Serving: *199 calories, 12g total fat, 5g sat fat, 11mg cholesterol, 147mg sodium, 22g carbohydrate, 2g fiber, 2g protein*

Lisa Ashton, Aston, PA

Chocolate Pinwheels

We love to serve this with warm spiced milk.

Serves 16

11-oz. tube refrigerated bread sticks
1/3 c. semi-sweet chocolate chips
1/4 c. butter, melted
1/2 c. sugar

Unroll bread sticks and cut them in half. Press chocolate chips in a single row along the top of each bread stick half; roll up into a pinwheel shape. Arrange pinwheels on a parchment paper-lined baking sheet. Brush with melted butter; sprinkle with sugar. Bake at 350 degrees for 10 to 12 minutes, until golden.

Nutrition Per Serving: *116 calories, 5g total fat, 3g sat fat, 8mg cholesterol, 241mg sodium, 18g carbohydrate, 1g fiber, 2g protein*

Chocolate Pinwheels

Ardith Field, Goldfield, IA

Dipped & Drizzled Pretzels

Make these sweet treats for any special holiday event and watch them disappear! Or wrap them up for a special gift!

Makes 5 cups, Serves 20

18-oz. pkg. white melting chocolate, divided
4 c. small pretzel twists
small amount pink paste food coloring

Melt 12 ounces white chocolate in a double boiler. Dip pretzels in melted chocolate and place on wax paper to harden. Melt remaining white chocolate in a small saucepan and tint pink; drizzle over pretzels. Allow to harden. Store in an airtight container.

Nutrition Per Serving: *174 calories, 8g total fat, 5g sat fat, 5mg cholesterol, 161mg sodium, 23g carbohydrate, 0g fiber, 3g protein*

Tiffany Leiter, Midland, MI

Speedy Peanut Butter Cookies

That's correct...there's no flour in these cookies!

Serves 15

1 c. sugar
1 c. creamy peanut butter
1 egg

Blend all ingredients together; set aside for 5 minutes. Scoop dough with a small ice cream scoop; place 2 inches apart on ungreased baking sheets. Make a crisscross pattern on top of each cookie using the tines of a fork; bake at 350 degrees for 10 to 12 minutes. Cool on baking sheets for 5 minutes; remove to wire rack to finish cooling.

Nutrition Per Serving: *158 calories, 9g total fat, 2g sat fat, 14mg cholesterol, 84mg sodium, 17g carbohydrate, 1g fiber, 5g protein*

Speedy Peanut Butter Cookies

Wendy Jacobs, Idaho Falls, ID

Apple-Gingerbread Cobbler

I like to serve this during the holidays, but my family actually asks for it all year long!

Serves 12

14-1/2 oz. pkg. gingerbread cake mix, divided
3/4 c. water
1/4 c. brown sugar, packed
1/2 c. butter, divided
Optional: 1/2 c. chopped pecans
2 21-oz. cans apple pie filling

Combine 2 cups gingerbread mix and water in a medium bowl; stir until smooth. Combine remaining gingerbread mix and brown sugar in a separate bowl, stirring to mix; cut in 1/4 cup butter with a pastry blender or fork until mixture is crumbly. Stir in pecans if using; set aside. Combine pie filling and remaining butter in a large saucepan; cook over medium heat for 5 minutes, or until thoroughly heated, stirring often. Spoon apple mixture evenly into a lightly greased 11"x 7" baking pan. Spoon gingerbread mixture over apple mixture; sprinkle with pecan mixture. Bake at 375 degrees for 30 to 35 minutes, until center is set.

Nutrition Per Serving: *334 calories, 13g total fat, 6g sat fat, 20mg cholesterol, 274mg sodium, 56g carbohydrate, 2g fiber, 2g protein*

Claire Bertram, Lexington, KY

Fruity Fresh Sorbet

Sorbet is so refreshing and easy to make. It is also low in calories and freezes well for a long time. Keep it on hand when friends drop by.

Makes 4 servings

1 peach, peeled, pitted and cubed
1 c. mango, peeled, pitted and cubed
1 ripe banana, peeled and mashed
4 T. water
1 T. lemon juice

Place fruit on a wax paper-lined baking sheet. Cover and freeze for about 2 hours, until completely frozen. Combine fruit, water and lemon juice in a food processor; process until smooth. Serve immediately, or spoon into a covered container and freeze up to 2 weeks.

Nutrition Per Serving: *68 calories, 0g total fat, 0g sat fat, 0mg cholesterol, 1mg sodium, 17g carbohydrate, 2g fiber, 1g protein*

GOOD TO KNOW
Mangoes are rich in potassium and vitamin C as well as pectin and fiber. Studies have shown that eating this yummy fruit regularly can help prevent heart disease and some cancers.

Fruity Fresh Sorbet

Sharon Jones, Oklahoma City, OK

Estelle's Baked Custard

So rich and creamy, this baked custard is a family favorite!

Serves 8

6 eggs
6 c. 2% milk
1/2 c. sugar
1-1/2 t. vanilla extract
1/8 t. salt
Garnish: whipped topping,
  cinnamon or nutmeg

Whisk eggs until well beaten in a large bowl. Add milk, sugar, vanilla and salt; whisk well. Pour into 8 ungreased custard cups. Set cups in a rimmed baking pan. Pour an inch of hot water into baking pan. Bake at 325 degrees for one hour, or until a knife inserted in center comes out clean. Garnish with whipped topping, cinnamon or nutmeg. Cool at room temperature or in refrigerator 1-1/2 to 2 hours before serving.

Nutrition Per Serving: *197 calories, 7g total fat, 3g sat fat, 154mg cholesterol, 177mg sodium, 22g carbohydrate, 0g fiber, 11g protein*

Lisa Ann Panzino-DiNunzio, Vineland, NJ

Chunky Applesauce

I love this recipe so I can make it in the slow cooker and have it ready to serve for a quick dessert.

Makes 8 servings

10 apples, peeled, cored and cubed
1/2 c. water
1/4 c. sugar
Optional: 1 t. cinnamon

Combine all ingredients in a slow cooker; toss to mix. Cover and cook on low setting for 6 to 8 hours. Serve warm or keep refrigerated in a covered container.

Nutrition Per Serving: *121 calories, 0g total fat, 0g sat fat, 0mg cholesterol, 0mg sodium, 32g carbohydrate, 3g fiber, 1g protein*

Chunky Applesauce

Lynda McCormick, Burkburnett, TX

Quick & Easy Lemon Bars

An even simpler way to make a super-simple dessert. These tasty treats are perfect for whipping up to take to bake sales or potlucks.

Serves 30

16-oz. pkg. angel food cake mix
22-oz. can lemon pie filling
Optional: chopped pecans,
   sweetened flaked coconut

Combine dry cake mix and pie filling in a large bowl; mix well. Spread in a greased 15"x10" jelly-roll pan; top with pecans or coconut, if desired. Bake at 350 degrees for 30 minutes. Let cool; cut into bars.

Nutrition Per Serving: *80 calories, 0g total fat, 0g sat fat, 2mg cholesterol, 125mg sodium, 18g carbohydrate, 0g fiber, 1g protein*

Michelle Rooney, Columbus, OH

Strawberry-Yogurt Mousse

A very easy-to-make, refreshing dessert I've made for many years... you'll love it!

Makes 10 servings

2 8-oz. containers strawberry
   yogurt
1/2 c. strawberries, hulled and
   crushed
8-oz. container frozen light whipped
   topping, thawed

Combine yogurt and strawberries; mix well. Fold in whipped topping; blend well. Spoon into cups or glasses. Place in refrigerator for 30 minutes before serving.

Nutrition Per Serving: *103 calories, 4g total fat, 3g sat fat, 4mg cholesterol, 44mg sodium, 14g carbohydrate, 0g fiber, 3g protein*

GOOD TO KNOW

Yogurt has both the nutritional value and the taste to make it one of the best foods out there. It contains a range of healthy nutrients such as calcium and vitamin B, all of which are necessary for good body function.

Strawberry-Yogurt Mousse

Charlene Smith, Lombard, IL

Coconut Clouds

For extra sparkle, top with a candied cherry and sprinkle with sugar before baking.

Serves 20

3/4 c. sugar
2-1/2 c. flaked coconut
2 egg whites, beaten
1 t. vanilla extract
1/8 t. salt

Combine all ingredients together. Beat with an electric mixer on medium-high speed until soft peaks form. Drop by tablespoonfuls, one inch apart, on a greased baking sheet; bake at 350 degrees for 15 to 20 minutes. Cool on a wire rack. Store in an airtight container.

Nutrition Per Serving: *80 calories, 3g total fat, 3g sat fat, 0mg cholesterol, 50mg sodium, 13g carbohydrate, 1g fiber, 1g protein*

Anita Williams, Pikeville, KY

Fresh Fruit Kabobs & Poppy Seed Dip

Try grilling these kabobs for a new spin. Place skewers over medium-high heat for 3 to 5 minutes...yum!

Makes 10 servings

6 c. fresh fruit like strawberries, kiwi, pineapple, honeydew and cantaloupe, peeled and cut into bite-size cubes or slices
8 to 10 wooden skewers

Arrange fruit pieces alternately on skewers. Serve Poppy Seed Dip alongside fruit kabobs.

POPPY SEED DIP:
1 c. vanilla yogurt
2 T. honey
4 t. lime juice
1 t. vanilla extract
1 t. poppy seed

Stir together ingredients in a small bowl. Keep chilled.

Nutrition Per Serving: *66 calories, 1g total fat, 0g sat fat, 1mg cholesterol, 25mg sodium, 15g carbohydrate, 1g fiber, 2g protein*

Fresh Fruit Kabobs & Poppy Seed Dip

Index

U.S. to Metric Recipe Equivalents

Volume Measurements

1/4 teaspoon . . . . 1 mL
1/2 teaspoon . . . . .2 mL
1 teaspoon . . . . .5 mL
1 tablespoon = 3 teaspoons . . . . 15 mL
2 tablespoons = 1 fluid ounce . . 30 mL
1/4 cup . . . . 60 mL
1/3 cup . . . . .75 mL
1/2 cup = 4 fluid ounces . . . . . .125 mL
1 cup = 8 fluid ounces . . . . 250 mL
2 cups=1 pint=16 fluid ounces 500 mL
4 cups =1 quart . . . . .75 mL

Weights

1 ounce . . . . .30 g
4 ounces. 120 g
8 ounces. . . . . .225 g
16 ounces = 1 pound . . . . 450 g

Baking Pan Sizes
Square
8x8x2 inches . . . . . 2 L = 20x20x5 cm
9x9x2 inches . . . . 2.5 L = 23x23x5 cm

Rectangular
13x9x2 inches. . . . 3.5 L = 33x23x5 cm
Loaf
9x5x3 inches . . . . . . 2 L = 23x13x7 cm

Round
8x1½ inches . . . . .1.2 L = 20x4 cm
9x1½ inches . . . . .1.5 L = 23x4 cm

Recipe Abbreviations

t. = teaspoon	ltr. = liter
T. = tablespoon	oz. = ounce
c. = cup	lb. = pound
pt. = pint	doz. = dozen
qt. = quart	pkg. = package
gal. = gallon	env. = envelope

Oven Temperatures

300° F . . . . 150° C
325° F . . . . 160° C
350° F . . . . 180° C
375° F . . . . 190° C
400° F . . . . 200° C
450° F . . . . .230° C

Kitchen Measurements

A pinch = 1/8 tablespoon
1 fluid ounce = 2 tablespoons
3 teaspoons = 1 tablespoon
4 fluid ounces = 1/2 cup
2 tablespoons = 1/8 cup
8 fluid ounces = 1 cup
4 tablespoons = 1/4 cup
16 fluid ounces = 1 pint
8 tablespoons = 1/2 cup
32 fluid ounces = 1 quart
16 tablespoons = 1 cup
16 ounces net weight = 1 pound
2 cups = 1 pint
4 cups = 1 quart
4 quarts = 1 gallon

Send us your favorite recipe

and the memory that makes it special for you!*

If we select your recipe for a brand-new **Gooseberry Patch** cookbook, your name will appear right along with it...and you'll receive a FREE copy of the book!

Submit your recipe on our website at

www.gooseberrypatch.com/sharearecipe

*Please include the number of servings and all other necessary information.

Have a taste for more?

Visit www.gooseberrypatch.com to join our Circle of Friends!

• Free recipes, tips and ideas plus a complete cookbook index
• Get mouthwatering recipes and special email offers delivered to your inbox.

You'll also love these cookbooks from **Gooseberry Patch**!

Autumn Recipes from the Farmhouse
Best Instant Pot Recipes
Church Potluck Favorites
Our Best Farm-Fresh Recipes
Fresh Farmhouse Recipes
Grandma's Best Comfort Foods
Made from Scratch
Our Best Quick & Easy Casseroles
Our Best Recipes in a Snap
A Year of Holidays

www.gooseberrypatch.com

Our Story

Back in 1984, our families were neighbors in little Delaware, Ohio. With small children, we wanted to do what we loved and stay home with the kids too. We had always shared a love of home cooking and so, **Gooseberry Patch** was born.

   Almost immediately, we found a connection with our customers and it wasn't long before these friends started sharing recipes. Since then we've enjoyed publishing hundreds of cookbooks with your tried & true recipes. We know we couldn't have done it without our

friends all across the country and we look forward to continuing to build a community with you. Welcome to the **Gooseberry Patch** family!

Jo Ann & Vickie